LET'S DANCE AND SING!

Freya Jaffke

Let's Dance and Sing!

Rhythmic Games for the Seasonal Year

Translated by Nina Kuettel
Illustrated by Christiane Lesch

WECAN
WALDORF EARLY CHILDHOOD
ASSOCIATION OF NORTH AMERICA

Let's Dance and Sing!
First English Edition
© 2016 Waldorf Early Childhood Association of North America
ISBN: 978-1-936849-36-9

Originally published in German as
Tanzt und singt!
Verlag Freies Geistesleben, Stuttgart
The text is taken from the 2003 edition,
the illustrations from the first edition (1987).

Text translated from the German by Nina Kuettel.
Except where otherwise indicated, all verses and song lyrics
have been translated for this volume by Nina Kuettel,
with revisions by Lory Widmer.

Published in the United States by the
Waldorf Early Childhood Association of North America
285 Hungry Hollow Road
Spring Valley, NY 10977
www.waldorfearlychildhood.org

Visit our online store at
store.waldorfearlychildhood.org

This publication is made possible through a grant from the Waldorf Curriculum Fund.

Contents

Note to the English Edition

The translation of this book involved a number of special challenges. In the chapter on compiling songs, verses, and games for the seasonal year, there were references to material from German sources, which are difficult or impossible to obtain in translation. We decided to substitute lists of similar seasonal material that is readily available in English, as a more useful resource for English-language readers. Many thanks to Nancy Foster for compiling these lists and also for proofreading and checking the entire manuscript.

The Christmas Play included references to several carols that would be very familiar to a German audience, and thus did not need written-out lyrics or music. These beautiful songs are probably not so familiar to English speakers, but we have included them in case you wish to make them a new part of your tradition. Where the *Oxford Book of Carols* could offer an existing translation, we have made use of it in the event that those words are already known to you. You may also wish to adapt the play to use different songs that your community knows better.

Elsewhere in the book, there are a few instances where alternate translations exist of some of the verses and circles. Where we were aware of these, they have been indicated in the text.

Lory Widmer
December 2016

Preface to the 2003 Edition

Joyfully dance and sing with your children and move to the beautiful rhythms of poems and melodies!

All parents and educators who are interested in providing their children with healthy education in movement should heed this call. Because of the widespread use of motorized vehicles, children are being pushed into mechanical processes of movement at an ever-increasing rate and earlier age. Even a walk in the woods is often ventured with the help of some kind of mechanical conveyance. Through sitting too long, while occupied with some kind of media, for example, children are sentenced to a state of "movement bottleneck."

Today, it is an open secret that it is becoming increasingly difficult for children, as well as adults, to find opportunities for unforced, meaningful, joyfully-enlivened movement accompanied by musical or spoken rhythms. Young children have a natural need to move in as many ways as possible, with games and imitative play, both indoors and outdoors. If we try to meet that need by using the examples and suggestions in this book, in a lively and artistic way, then we are nourishing the childhood impulse that urges children into creative and meaningful activity.
 With this goal in mind, may *Let's Dance and Sing!* find its way to the bookshelves of many more families and children's groups; and may it be a helpful companion for adults.

Freya Jaffke
Spring 2003

Preface to the First Edition

We hope that this book on the subject of rhythmic games and their appropriate use with young children will be a help to all educators who are new to early childhood teaching. Young parents might also find suggestions on how to bring songs and poems into the home, especially when it comes to the difficult task of finding appropriate gestures and movements to go along with them. The chapter about preparation for rhythmic games and the different elements they contain might be particularly helpful in this regard. The examples given in the second part of the book could also help stimulate ideas for coming up with one's own gestures. However, it is still advisable, for example, to carefully observe how a mother rocks her baby in her arms, or folds the laundry; how a gardener uses a rake or hoe, how a toad hops, how the wind blows through the trees, or a flower bud opens. An inner connection with such processes can enliven one's own imagination. In this way, gestures may be found that teach children something about the truth contained in our living surroundings.

The directions given for playing the games evolved over time as the games were played. They are not set in stone and are only intended to be suggestions. Working with the games over a longer period of time and considering the special characteristics of particular groups of children, will always lead to slight changes and variations.

It is very satisfying to children when familiar, seasonal songs and poems are brought out again. They have rested in the children's souls and grown with them. Often, some external event will prompt a fragment of a memory and these songs and poems will be joyfully greeted like good friends. New songs and poems can be introduced without any difficulty.

With the songs, we mainly try to give preference to melodies in the pentatonic scale. Their free and open nature, which does not compel a keynote (they are not shaped by a major or minor key) gives young children a chance to sing with lighthearted, cheerful exhilaration, and also to listen. Therapeutically speaking, this is very important. Children today are constantly exposed to levels of noise, be it from traffic or some other technology, which make it difficult for them to ever really feel calm.

If we choose to use familiar, traditional songs at Christmas time, it is done only after taking into consideration the children's family situations. During this time of year, at least, many families still do sing together.

For those of you who have had only a few years of experience with this type of rhythmic play, you will soon notice that older children in a mixed-age group, during periods of free play, will often reach back to certain aspects of rhythmic play they experienced earlier, completely on their own initiative. They will either invite younger children to join in with some game and play together very freely, or they might include younger ones in a little table-top puppet theater, or a story about a doll's birthday. In this way, the games become valuable assets for children, parents and educators. They enrich children's creative play, as well as the activities of adults, in a very special way.

To all my colleagues and friends who helped me create this book, I extend my heartfelt gratitude.

Freya Jaffke
January 1987

The Importance of Rhythmic Games

One of the most important tasks of Waldorf early childhood education is to bring life itself, the activities of life, into the classroom. The question is: In what form should it be brought, so that it is accepted by the children and carried into their play? Rhythmic games are one of the many tools that help us achieve this goal. Daily life is able to unfold in artistically formed processes of movement.

Some of these processes are hardly seen any more by children, for example gestures of work such as sowing seeds, shoeing horses, or making shoes. Through rhythmic games, these activities are very intensely experienced and often stimulate the themes of free play, both indoors and out. However, this effect will be created only if adults, with all the energy and radiant joy they can muster, are successful in inspiring the children's enthusiasm for the archetypal gestures of activities like sowing seeds, mowing with a scythe, or threshing grain. Otherwise, it could easily happen that one of the six-year-old boys might suddenly get the idea to imitate the sound of a motor and run around the room in stereotypical "driving" movements and declare he is doing the work with a combine harvester.

If we are intensively occupied with the development of young children and do not close our eyes to the fact that movement development is increasingly endangered, we will come to the following conclusion: It makes sense to bring children into movement through rhythmic poems and songs that have to do with traditional processes of human work activities. At the same time, energetic and imaginative movement in this way is very healing for children.

During the first few years of school, these activities are newly enlivened if there is a school farm or garden. It provides a good basis for later understanding the mechanics of the machinery that has replaced so much of human work activity in so many areas of life.

Thanking the shoemaker for the finished shoes, greeting others and dancing together, marveling at the abundance of sheaves when the harvest wagon is loaded, rocking a baby, everything that we are familiar with in terms of relationships or social behaviors, can be introduced and cultivated through rhythmic games. The same applies when it comes to human relationships to the animal, plant, and mineral kingdoms. The loving attention shown to a horse, how the owner cares for it and then rides it, or the care that a shepherd shows for his sheep; love for a little snail slowly crawling along, or the birds and insects that fill the air; and feeling one's way into the processes of plant growth, blooming and bearing fruit — these are all very important formative elements. Thus human beings can feel and maintain an inner sense of connectedness with the natural environment in an artistic way. Seasonal celebrations and holidays are special highlights. The spiritual background of the yearly festivals flows into the presentations. Naturally, children do not have an intellectual understanding of this.

This particular kind of rhythmic activity is closely associated with a young child's joy in self-directed movement. Activity and movement of all kinds form one of the main elements in which a child lives. Children have an innate ability to imitate, which makes it easy for them to slip into all transparent processes and absorb the movement impulses found there. During *free play*, children are able to experience such impulses in the appropriate intensity, at their own speed and self-determined length of time. While playing *rhythmic games* as a group, children come to the same experiences, but in this case they are led by the gestures which adults have chosen to accompany the songs and poems (see the section on "Preparation").

This has nothing to do with inserting contrived or artificial movements into the process, but rather, with learned consistency between movement and speech. All processes of movement have a deeply penetrating effect on the subtle, inner differentiation of a child's organism. That is why all human movements that are consciously performed and experienced are especially important — for example, activities in the household or garden, a craftsman's work, artistic gestures as described above, and also many processes in nature.

Such impressions from the living surroundings are absorbed into a child's life energy. This has a health-promoting effect and offers a balance to the impressions made by mechanical processes from the realm of technology. Furthermore, artistically formed movements help cultivate the elements of language and music. (Again, see "Preparation.")

A child is able to absorb all of this into her growth and development processes during the phase of physical development. Awareness of this will make adults conscious of their great responsibility in this regard. With an overview of children's developmental phases and the universal principles behind them, adults will try to find the right measure of activity and the way to model such activities.

Compiling Poems, Songs, Games, and Dances for the Seasonal Year

The following considerations are meant only as suggestions for selecting material from the large amount available and are in no way exclusive or complete. Every teacher, parent, or caregiver will very soon find her own way of creatively handling things, whether in her daily work in a kindergarten, or anywhere groups of children are gathered for special events, like birthday parties, festivals, or family vacations.

You will find, more and more, that the best way to make a connection between the songs and poems is by first gaining a general overview of the seasonal year. When you are aware of the qualities and activities of the seasons throughout the year, material suitable for individual months, or even weeks, will emerge.

Let us first take a look at a few of the factors in connection with this process that really stand out and lead us to the following question: What happens with the earth, plants and animals during the course of a whole year?

If we concentrate our thoughts on the great rhythm of the earth and its interaction with the sun, we see that plants awaken in the spring and have their most intensive blooming season in the summer. In the autumn they bear fruit and the winter brings a slow withdrawal of life forces. What an abundance of different processes are there before us! Additionally, there are the effects of the elements, such as rain, sunshine, wind, storms, thunderstorms, frost, and snow, along with those helpful elemental spirits known as undines, sylphs, salamanders, gnomes, giants, and fairies.

If we turn our attention to the animal kingdom, we see how the animals slowly awaken from their winter rest and can be observed in increasing variety up to the height of summer. In the autumn, some animals prepare for the winter, while others go into hibernation.

After this short overview of the seasons of the year, we come to a second factor and these questions: Where do human beings stand within the process of the seasons? What activities do human beings perform on earth that are connected with the seasons of the year? What cultural functions are human beings obliged to fulfill in this regard?

Related to this factor, we have the appearance of a variety occupations and trades, such as farmer, gardener, shepherd, fisher, shoemaker, carpenter, blacksmith, laundress, and mother, for example.

Another question has to do with how the Christian festivals are interwoven with the natural course of the seasons in places with a temperate climate. This question demands an especially serious effort and continuous, patient and penetrating work. There is not room within the scope of this book to go into further details on the subject (see "Further Reading").

If we begin our search for songs and poems while keeping the above considerations in mind, we will soon discover some beautiful material. Above all, we should make sure that with regard to the content of a rhythmic game, one thing always leads into another, so that something like a little story is created each time. Naturally, we always need short connecting or transitional words, especially with unfamiliar material, either between poems and songs, or between repetitions, especially when new elements are introduced (see "Elements of Rhythmic Games").

When choosing material, especially poems, make sure that the material lends itself to the addition of an ample amount of meaningful gestures. There are many great poems and verses that have more of a narrative quality, which makes them unsuitable for rhythmic games. A young child must always be able to immediately imitate the human activity or movement of an animal that is being presented because that is how the child makes a direct inner connection with it. Indicative or descriptive gestures are therefore only occasionally useful.

Whether the language element or the musical element is more prominent in a circle game is not an important factor. The content of the material will determine which element is more pronounced.

Having one theme carried over throughout the year can be a help when putting together material. We begin at the start of a new school year in the autumn.

Remember, after the summer vacation there are usually a few new faces and they have to slowly become used to a new situation. A very short circle game would be in order, such as the following:

Mother Bird (an adult) flies around (with arms spread wide) with all her little bird children and sings "Aye, my little bird" (see music on next page).

Then everyone flies back to the nest and has a nice long rest. "In the morning, with the smiling Sun, all are awake, every one."

A. Künstler; Words translated by E. Moore-Haas

Aye, my lit – tle bird, Spread your shin – ing wings,

Bring my child__ sun__ shine, Aye,__ my__ lit – tle bird.

This is repeated a few times. It leads the children in a gentle way into the activity of imitation.

The same thing can be done with the song, "We open now the pigeon house." To begin, we squat down in the middle with all the children, nestle our head a little under our arm and say: "Coo-coo-ri-coo, coo-coo-ri-coo; close the pigeon house door, please do."

Then we open our arms and "fly" around while singing the song. At the end, everyone is back inside the "pigeon house" and it begins again.

A. Künstler

The Journey through the Year

For our journey through the seasons, songs and poems were chosen as examples that are tried and true favorites. Even so, they are still only suggestions which you may or may not decide to use to create your own rhythmic games. Note that we do not repeat all of the poems, verses and songs every year and in the same order. Being together with the children is really a living process, out of which so many new and beautiful things are created. We only have to be flexible enough to listen to what is coming toward us from the children. We should take notice if feelings of dissatisfaction arise, especially from the older children, which we might be able to bypass imaginatively through small variations in our game. Such subtle interventions are hard to put into words because they have to be continuously examined and refined.

Therefore, the following items should really only be taken as a general framework.

For the English edition, songs and verses available in English-language books have been chosen as suggestions to supplement the material translated for this volume. The numbers in parentheses refer to the list of sources found at the end of this section.

Autumn

By the end of August and the beginning of September, the high point of summer has passed and the time of harvest is getting closer. There is still an abundance of flowers blooming, but perhaps the children are already experiencing herbs being harvested and dried, or fall fruits being picked and processed or dried for the winter. Out of this atmosphere, the rhythmic games slowly begin to reflect the activities of harvest— from mowing fields of grain to baking bread; from shaking the fruit trees to carrying the fruit home in baskets, and, of course, pulling carrots out of the ground in the garden.

Rhythmic Games for Harvest Time – see pages 38-45 in this volume
Autumn Has Come (source 7) p. 35
Rosy Apples Grow (5) p. 41
Here's a little apple tree. . . (7) p. 39
Father Sun Helps Make the Wheat (1) p. 10
Haying Circle Play (4) p. 4
The Harvest Time Again is Here (7) p. 16
See the Golden Grain (1) p. 7
The farmer gave us golden grain. . . (8) p. 37
Bread (2) p. 45

Michaelmas

During harvest time and the transition from the bright, luminous high summer season to the darker season of autumn, a very special event takes place on September 29: Michaelmas, the festival of St. Michael (see "Further Reading").

Michaelmas Circle (source 6) p. 45
Michael, Michael (6) p. 58
Michaël, Michaël (7) p. 30
Wind in the Wood (7) p. 29

Late Autumn

After the harvest festival, around the beginning of October, the first autumn winds are already blowing the leaves off the trees. In the rustling of the fallen leaves, we accompany the animals as they prepare for their winter sleep, such as hedgehogs, for example. We gather winter provisions with the mice and squirrels. Sunlight is noticeably less bright. The sun gives us a small gift of light that we may now carry around in lanterns held before us. The St. Martin motif resounds in the lantern songs. Understanding for this motif will be accessible to the children in later years.

At this time of year, life in nature withdraws under the surface of the earth. Here we meet the industrious gnomes and we diligently work right along with them. The giant also makes his appearance, as an element of polarity; somewhat slow and clumsy, perhaps. Through the giant, we are in turn provided with many dynamic and joyful elements.

Giants and Gnomes – see pages 46-50
Lantern Songs – pages 50-51
It is Fall Time (source 2) p. 9
In the Autumn Garden (5) p. 16
I'm the Wind (5) p. 16
When Mary Goes Walking (3) p. 19
Little Cricket (4) p. 8
Acorns Falling (4) p. 6
Over Branches (4) p. 9
Come Little Leaves (7) p. 41
Autumn winds are sighing. . . (7) p. 45
Wee Dwarfs (3) p. 14
Dwarf Circle Play (4) p. 21
Behold the giant big and strong. . . (8) p. 66
When Every Earthly Creature Sleeps (4) p. 11
Golden Sun is Going Down (4) p. 13
The Sunlight Fast is Dwindling (7) p. 26
My Lantern (7) p. 26

Advent

During the time of Advent, when it is steadily becoming darker outside, an adult should try to allow his or her soul to become increasingly brighter and quieter. Children will experience the same thing through festive events, such as the Advent Garden, for example, not so much through the intellect, but much more through what they perceive through the senses, which are activated by the physical activity.

Within the framework of this book, we are not able to go into detail about these events. However, in regard to circle games, the character of St. Nicholas is at the forefront. He comes to the children as the herald of the approaching Christ Child. On his way from heaven down to earth he meets the forest animals: birds, elk, deer and rabbits. This is the theme of the song "From Heavenly Castle Heights," found on page 53 in this volume. It lends itself easily to circle games and is especially appropriate for the first week of Advent.

After St. Nicholas, the Christmas Play begins, which we play at the end of the morning, every day (see page 54). During this one-and-a-half to two-week period, we dispense with the rhythmic game before the morning snack, so the children do not get overtired. In this way, they are able to calmly become immersed in this central, pivotal event.

Nicholas, St. Nicholas (source 4) p. 15
In the Advent Garden (9) p. 15
Softly, Softly (9) p. 16
Then Wished our Mother Mary (9) p. 19
Shepherds, Shepherds (4) p. 15
From Heaven's Arch So High (6) p. 104
While the Stars are Shining Bright (6) p. 102
Poems for the Midwinter (Advent) Garden (6)
  p. 91

Epiphany and Wintertime/Carnival

The Three Kings Play occurs after Christmas (see page 70). Like the Christmas Play, it is used to end the kindergarten morning. We try to carry it through to the end of January, or even to Candlemas on February 2. It is quite a short play. We are able to resume the rhythmic games before the morning snack at the same time. Now, in our rhythmic game, we let it snow, ride on horse-drawn sleighs, get covered with snow under the hazelnut bush with three sparrows and, in the end, come to the frozen lake where the fish below bump against the icy surface. But the sun is slowly getting warmer, the lake thaws and the agile trout play their lively, splashing games. Then the fisherman arrives. He is followed gradually by other merry tradespeople, especially Cobbler Leatherfine (see page 86). Games based on various trades and work activities lead us into Carnival time. On Carnival Day, all the children come to kindergarten in costume, dressed as some kind of tradesperson. Then we work and dance like the merry tradespeople.

Winter songs and verses – see pages 78-81
Work songs and games – pages 82-91, and
   dances on pages 105-109
In the Winter Garden (source 9) p. 42
Three Kings (4) p. 16
At the Manger (9) p. 37
Snow (2) p. 13
Snow is Piling up so High (1) p. 29
Cross-Patch (2) p. 17
Come, Little Snowflakes (4) p. 19
Winter Circle (5) p. 19
Chip, Chop (9) p. 56
Sail, fishing boat. . . (8) p. 62
Fresh fish for sale. . . (8) p. 52
The knife grinder. . . (8) p. 53
Today is the fair. . . (8) p. 53
Brown buns to sell. . . (8) p. 57
Down the hill. . . (8) p. 56
The Carpenter's Hammer (1) p. 31
Needle Bright (1) p. 36

Early Spring

After Carnival, we bring the horse out of the barn again, the same one that keeps popping up at different times throughout the year. We have the horse shod, go out for a ride, jump, trot, and snort along. We come upon the first snails that have awakened from their winter's sleep, and soon the rabbits, as well.

The Blackmith – see page 80
Where To, Where To, You Little Gnome?
   – page 52
My little pony needs a pair of shoes. . .
   (source 5) p. 41
Pitty, patty, polt. . . (5) p. 41
Ride a Cock-Horse (8) p. 83
A Farmer Went Trotting (8) p. 85
Saddle my pony free. . . (8) p. 45
Sleep, You Little Willow (4) p. 23
Little Snail (10) p. 42
Pitter, Patter, Raindrops (5) p. 23
Winter's Past (4) p. 24
Snow Drop (10) p. 16
Late Winter Circle (5) p. 22
Early Spring Circle (5) p. 25
My Lady Spring (10) p. 21

Spring

Once again, the helpful gnomes are directing the activities underground. We pay a visit to "Knack, the Gnome" (see page 92). He picks a little flower for a joyful spring celebration and all the forest animals share in his happiness. Soon, the first little violets are blooming in the garden, in expectation of Easter.

The first week after Easter, we play the "Easter Bunnies," who are busily painting colorful eggs and hiding them. Then we become in turn the "children" who hunt for eggs (see page 94). This is also when work begins again in the fields. The seed sower spreads his seeds over the field and the "maidens" plant flower and herb seeds in the garden.

Rain and sunshine help the plants grow and develop. Each day we immerse ourselves in the gestures of sowing, planting, sprouting, growing, blooming, rain and sunshine.

Spring songs and games – see pages 92-97
Clip-de-clap (source 3) p. 18
Come, Oh Come, Ye Little Gnomes (10) p. 30
Planting Circle (5) p. 28
Your rake and shovel. . . (10) p. 47
In the Easter Garden (10) p. 33
Easter Rabbit (4) p. 25
Spring Circle (5) p. 35
22   *Mother Earth* (10) p. 46

Summer

During the season that includes Whitsun, all the various kinds of birds play a big role. A mother bird flies out and brings back food for her babies; Mrs. Twitterling, the chickadee, finds a little breadcrumb, and gulls fly over expansive fields.

When the sun reaches its zenith and all of nature has reached the pinnacle of development, and light and warmth fill the air, then butterflies flutter from flower to flower, bees gather pollen and beetles appear in colorful variety. It is all expressed beautifully in the song "A Summer Feast" (see page 101) which may be sung for the summer solstice celebration (Feast of St. John the Baptist).

During the rest of the midsummer season, we wander with the shepherd through the meadows. In the nighttime, he observes the little fireflies and watches the fairies dance. Sometimes, he is surprised by a summer thunderstorm. At midday, he might come across a little gnome gathering berries, who then falls asleep and is surprised by the Midday Witch (see page 102). In the midst of all these midsummer happenings, we spare a little time for the summer festival dances.

Summer songs, verses, and games – see pages 98-103

Thunderstorm game – page 38

Festival dances:

Wooden Shoe Dance – pages 108-109

The Jolly Jumper – page 110

Johnny Fiddler – page 106

Come, Let's All Be Dancing – page 105

Bumble Bee (source 4) p. 28

Waken, Sleeping Butterfly (10) p. 36

Butterfly (5) p. 36

White Sheep (2) p. 55

In May I Go A-Walking (11) p. 22

Maypole Dance (4) p. 27

When woods awake. . . (4) p. 30

Little Mary Wine-cups (11) p. 47

Late Spring Circle (5) p. 41

King Sun (11) p. 28

High, high in the bright blue sky. . . (5) p. 45

Larky, larky, larky, lee. . . (5) p. 45

One Bright and Sunny Morning (5) p. 46

Shepherd Maiden (5) p. 63

Summer Showers (11) p. 24

The Thunder is Growling (5) p. 37

There Was a Little Rose (11) p. 48

Saint John (11) p. 30

Tomorrow is Midsummer Day (11) p. 33

Sources:

1. Karen Lonsky, *A Day Full of Song* (WECAN, 2009)
2. Channa Seidenberg, *I Love to be Me* (Wynstones Press, 2002)
3. Johanne Russ, *Clump-a-Dump and Snickle-Snack*, (Mercury Press)
4. Nancy Foster, ed., *Let Us Form a Ring*, (Acorn Hill, distributed by WECAN)
5. Nancy Foster, ed., *Dancing as We Sing*, (Acorn Hill, distributed by WECAN)
6. Nancy Foster, ed., *The Seasonal Festivals in Early Childhood: Seeking the Universally Human*, (WECAN, 2010)
7. Wynstones Press, *Autumn* (Wynstones, 1999)
8. Wynstones Press, *Spindrift* (Wynstones, 1999)
9. Wynstones Press, *Winter* (Wynstones, 1999)
10. Wynstones Press, *Spring* (Wynstones, 1999)
11. Wynstones Press, *Summer* (Wynstones, 1999)

Transitions from One Theme to Another

We begin by collecting a few songs and poems so that, on a daily basis, one thing or another is repeated (perhaps with variations) many times. For instance, a cheerful little fish is playing in the waves; first, the very little ones, and then the very big ones, follow along. Or, a gnome takes a different little hammer with him every time he goes to a different mountain in order to hammer out different kinds of precious minerals. This process can be repeated over a period of days, perhaps even a whole week. But on the days the children have eurythmy, there should be a break from the rhythmic games because both together would definitely be too much.

The transition to a new theme can proceed smoothly by gradually introducing something of the new theme into whatever you are currently doing. In order to accomplish this, you will have to leave something out of the current theme and replace it with something from the new theme. You will soon be able to sense within yourself, and from the children, the best way to go about it. Certainly, there are times of year when completely new material may be introduced without a transitional period because it is determined by vacation times or seasonal festivals.

Those who are new to this work may find it difficult in the beginning to become comfortable with the repetitions. These have to be enlivened and approached in a new way all the time (see also "Elements of Rhythmic Games," page 30). Working with the children and seeing their constantly renewed joy in the repeated rhythmic games will help you get through any beginner's difficulties.

Preparation for Rhythmic Games

Enjoyment, lightness and cheeriness are the major elements that contribute to the basic mood of these games. But when we speak of joy, we mean the joy created by the thing itself and its careful preparation, and not the joy that can come to us from the outside, through a special occasion or event.

Adopting and/or adapting songs and poems also allows us to discover differentiated movements that go along with them. The movements should be well rehearsed and you should have good mastery of them before introducing them to the children. It is a good idea to allow yourself plenty of preparation time so that you become very sure of the words, melody and movements. This makes it easier for the children to find their way into the game.

How to Handle Imitation

It is advisable to frequently call to mind how imitation is currently taking place in the group. In working with children, we can trust in their ability to imitate. This ability begins to change around age eight. However, today, a child's natural ability to imitate requires special care and attention. Through the influence of outside circumstances, many children's ability for imitation is severely weakened. The first thing we should do is become totally aware of the process of imitation and then we should try to enliven the process within ourselves through practice. In this way, we will gradually "get a handle on it." When imitation is supposed to take place, there has to be something there beforehand. Grasped correctly, this "beforehand" consists of a mere few seconds of time

The length of time is really not the issue. The important thing is to give children the opportunity of a moment of "breathing-in" that which is to be imitated. They grasp it with their own will and externalize it through movement. What makes up this important moment? It consists of one thing only: a gesture of movement. *An adult leads with a gesture just slightly before speaking or singing.* For example, you would spread your arms, preparing for a bird to fly, hold the position for a moment and then begin with the words of a text or a song, before "flapping your wings." It is a subtlety that is not easy to sense, and yet it is strongly effective and forms the basis for healthy imitation. At first, you will need to keep this front and center in your awareness, for as long as it takes to become an automatic habit.

If you lack confidence with this, or need more detail than has been presented here, it is a good idea to turn to an experienced colleague and practice together. All individual effort in this area will be rewarded, as the children are able to imitate with increasing concentration and also experience more joy while doing so. In this way, you will be able to strengthen children's ability to imitate, which is sometimes lacking. We really should not challenge children who have weak imitative faculties to improve; rather, we should wait (sometimes for months) until the impulse to imitate awakens in them. However, if you are dealing with mischief-makers, then, of course, you will have to react appropriately (see also the section on "Behavioral and Pedagogical Issues").

Gestures of Adults

Every movement we use in a presentation should be performed with inner participation. The children need to sense that we are engaged with our whole being. It is also beneficial if the movement originates from exact observation of a human task or work activity, the characteristic movement of an animal, or some process in nature, which will make it seem compelling and real. Certainly, in some cases it will be necessary to go out and try to find people who still know how to use a threshing flail, sow seed in a field, or mow with a scythe. You should transform such tasks (and many others) into rhythmic, dynamic gestures. Generally speaking, you can be very sparing with the gestures, as illustrated by the examples in the second part of this book.

It is really not necessary to have a different movement for each line of text. It is better to move less, while making each movement count to the fullest. Too much movement can create stress. Less movement allows the children to join in with joyful ease. Often, one kind of movement is plenty for a whole stanza; for instance, the little horse goes slowly at first, starts trotting in the second verse and finally, runs to the barn at the end. The same is true of a gnome gathering strawberries, or a snail creeping through the grass.

It is assumed that gestures and words rhythmically correspond with each other. Since younger children (preschoolers) still need word-linked rhythms, when we hammer, clap, or ring a bell, for example, we keep to the rhythm of the syllables. Depending on their age level, the children will move along as they are able and we leave them completely free in their movements. Children's desire to keep the rhythm of syllables awakens more and more as they get closer to school age.

Gestures in Circle Games and Eurythmy

Teachers who are a little familiar with the art of eurythmy will find it easier to move in the ways indicated. However, you should always keep in mind that there is a difference between eurythmy gestures and those used in circle games. Eurythmy gestures correspond to the impulses created by sound and speech formation, which work in all processes of becoming, and their creation is based upon the experience of the soul/spiritual quality of music and speech. In contrast, the gestures for circle games are based upon the connection between human beings and things like the natural environment and human social/cultural activity. These gestures always have to do with imitation of an external activity, such as using a scythe, work activities in trades and crafts, an animal running, greeting or thanking another person, or recreating a perceived form — the moon or a basket. Meanwhile, it may appear as if eurythmy gestures are being used in a round-dance game. This is simply due to the nature of the thing being imitated

and is justified for that reason. For example, when a fish is tussling with the waves, you have the movement of the waves in your mind's eye. You are not thinking of the formative forces of sound and speech that are active in the waves. Nevertheless, the same forces are at work in the gesture, which is used for two different purposes. For a kindergarten teacher, the impulses originate in the experience and imitation of a natural process, but a eurythmy teacher is dealing with the added elements of the principles of sound and speech formation, both in her awareness and in her artistic practice. Incorrectly mixing eurythmy with circle games will not occur as long as a kindergarten teacher remains focused on performing the external action that corresponds with the song or poem, whereas a eurythmy teacher is dedicated to the soul/spiritual principles of sound and speech formation. Eurythmy is actually visible song and speech.

Speech of Adults

Your speech should sound as natural as possible: calm, sunny, and in a normal tone of voice. Good breath control and clear pronunciation will allow you to bring variety to the joy of speaking. However, you should avoid the use of theatrical effects with your voice. Children react to such things in one of two ways: fear or fascination in younger children, and perhaps amusement in older children. Either way, it distracts from the true essence of a thing. All the same, it is possible to express the character of something by placing special emphasis on the consonants, for example with words like rumble, scurry, rustle, or hop. If you are unsure of the text or have not thought it out in advance, the children will have a tendency to start misbehaving. Total familiarity with the verses and poems frees you from depending on a written text and instead allows you to concentrate on the children. It will immediately cause the children to feel protected by you and they will joyfully join in with the activity. If at some point a line really is forgotten, you can probably easily find another rhyme on the spur of the moment.

We always allow the children to live in the game without *requiring* them to speak or sing along. They are not consciously aware of whether they are singing or speaking along with us, provided we do not call their attention to it. Often, children who seldom speak or sing along in the kindergarten will repeat everything at home with amazing accuracy, which shows that they are intensively receiving everything.

Singing of Adults

Whenever you sing with young children, you should make sure that the songs are not pitched too low. The normal range for a young child's voice encompasses two fifth intervals; that is, from the D above middle C to the E in the next octave. In accordance with a young child's development, we should favor songs that are in the pentatonic scale. It is important that the songs contain a certain freshness and lightness. The tempo should not drag, but rather should correspond more to the faster pulse of a child. But this does not mean we should hurry through the songs. We are always confronted with the difficult task of finding the right tempo. This also applies to the volume. A diffident singing voice or a full-throated one would be equally out of place.

Finally, it should be pointed out that rhythmic games involve learning how to do an artistic activity in very differentiated ways. Just as with every art form, continuous effort in the various areas presented is essential. However, more and more, it will develop into an ability. And so, with time, the detailed, preparatory steps we take before doing an activity with the children will no longer need to be front and center in our awareness and we will be freer in our pedagogical tasks.

Form of Rhythmic Games

When we earnestly work with children's faculty of imitation, the first form for rhythmic games that will come about is a loosely formed group. While singing or speaking, the adult moves clockwise around the circle. The children follow along, more or less close by, each on her own path. They are left completely free when it comes to tempo, length of steps, path walked, and whether they choose to walk more on the inside of the circle or the outside. The age of a child and her ability to imitate are closely related and this has to be taken fully into consideration. Out of her own free impulse, every child learns to insert herself into the movement process. There is no external organizational impulse that can awaken a child from her dream-like devotion to an activity. It happens repeatedly that one of the three-year-old children will stand still, either in awe or daydreaming, while the other children simply pass by or move around him. Or, a younger child might move along while standing very close to an adult, perhaps even holding on to her skirt. In contrast, five- and six-year-old children have much more conscious awareness when they follow along. They usually require a lot of room and will likely choose the longest and widest path. Wisely chosen songs and poems, in conjunction with the dynamic elements of rhythmic games, will cause a circle to form for seconds at a time every once in a while. But the circle will disintegrate again immediately because its formation stems from movement and not a prescribed form. As adults, it is not really possible to demonstrate a circle form. The ability to form a circle and maintain it requires a special awareness, not only for the form, but also for one's neighbors to the left and right. We can make use of the circle form only sparingly because this ability will naturally awaken in children with the change of teeth and become like second nature to them.

When we work with children in a circle, or move with them in a circular motion, we are integrating ourselves into all the cosmic movement in our surroundings, of the sun and the stars, for example. It has a stimulating effect on children's life forces.

Naturally, it is perfectly fine to play rhythmic games every so often that are based on being in a circle. It will be easier if you wait until the second half of the school year, when the youngest children are very used to things and the older children support them. Even so, we still do not require the children to simply stand in a circle, but instead, we take two children by the hand and wait until a few other children do likewise, and in this way the circle closes.

Forming a circle also depends on whether there are too many children in the group who like to tug and pull when someone takes their hand, or are not able to hold the circle. If you try to work mostly with a loosely formed group, you will be pleased to find how experience will help you discover the mysterious processes involved in imitation. You will also realize that sporadically, for a few short moments, a circle comes about almost effortlessly.

Elements of Rhythmic Games

Joy and cheerfulness are the main elements in the activity of rhythmic games. The games are infused with a living dynamic, with diligent, happy activity and, occasionally, earnest, ceremonious moments. All of the different elements (especially the polarities of fast/slow, bold/cautious, large/small, rumbling/rustling, frivolity/seriousness and vigorous/gentle) are embedded within a single context. The way you implement them is through repetitions of single lines of text, or a couple of lines, a whole poem, or single stanzas. For instance, if you have just done a "thunderstorm" (see Rhythmic Games for Harvest Time on page 38), you could continue with a very strong storm by making the gestures correspondingly larger and more energetic, or perhaps even louder. A very tiny little hint of a thunderstorm would come at the end, when practically nothing could be heard. Another example: Gnomes are inside a mountain cave, hammering first with their little golden hammers, then with their little silver hammers, or perhaps with an especially thick and heavy hammer. The gnomes scurry away and a giant stomps into the cave with great, rumbling steps.

Still another example is found in the Pigeon House game, described on page 16, where we constantly alternate between "open" and "expanded" and "contracted" and "tight."

If we manage to make a connection with the unique way of being of the different elements, and that connection has enough intensity and joy, so that it seems like a great breath is wafting through the whole of the activity, then the children will happily and devotedly follow us. However, we have to make sure that we do not change from one element to another too quickly. The children really need to be able to become immersed in the game. Changing too rapidly, without even a short pause, is very stimulating and will make the children feel rather more restless than harmonious. When transitioning from one element of movement to another, especially the first few times, it is helpful if an adult says something that leads into the next element. Through the different elements, rhythmic games are always infused with an arc of dramatic tension created by contrasting movements, by holding in and letting go. This is really the one fundamental element that permeates not only individual songs and poems, but circle games and dances as a whole. The children are carefully led from one polarity to another, which allows individual children to find inner harmony. Naturally, the repetition of activities from day to day is a great help.

Differentiation, Roles, Costumes

A young child is able to come to terms with different situations and roles naturally and with a great degree of inner flexibility. This is the ability we work with in rhythmic games. Naturally, adults have to create and maintain within themselves a natural freshness and flexibility as well.

When we are working with a newly formed group of children, as is usually the case at the beginning of a school year, or at family children's parties, initially it is best if all the children do the same thing in a rhythmic game. It is absolutely no problem for the children if they first play the blacksmith who shoes the horse and then play the horse, for example, or, first the snail slowly creeping along and then the lively child who likes to run fast, or the gnome in the mountain and the next moment the giant.

When the same games are played over a period of days and the children become very familiar with them, we can begin to make differentiations in various small groups. However, it is only necessary to do this if you have the impression that the older children need something more. The "more" might simply consist of an adult bringing nuances into the different elements of the game, or introducing some small, new element. If you wish to assign "roles," it is recommended to always assign different roles to small groups instead of to individual children. It is also better to avoid putting one child alone in the middle. A small group will make the children feel secure and protected.

Those who wish to become very acquainted with the faculty of imitation in children will do well to leave out costumes in most cases. The children hardly need them. At every moment, they are the character being played. Their faculty of imitation gives them a very deep connection with the respective roles. There are exceptions, of course: The Christmas Play and the Three Kings Play and perhaps also for a specific occasion that includes circle dances.

Behavioral and Pedagogical Issues

Whenever difficulties arise in connection with a rhythmic game, the first thing we should do is ask ourselves the following: Was it presented in such a way that all of the different age groups could be engaged without being overtaxed? Was I very sure of the texts and melodies? Were my own movements well thought out and confidently performed? Was the tempo too quick, or perhaps boring? Were there enough repetitions, but also not too many? Was I projecting joy in the activity, as well as the necessary lightness?

After the answers to these questions have been examined, we turn our attention to the children and try to calmly call to mind all the circumstances of the difficulty. Does the problem seem to be originating with a specific child? Does this child act out at other times during the day, or have special challenges? Does the child find it hard to calm down, always talking or fidgeting? In other words, is it hard for the child to forget about being restless when involved in imitation activity? Does the child purposely act foolish by treading on someone's feet, poking someone in the back, or even trying to trip another child, for example? Or, does the child clown around in an attempt to draw the other children's attention and incite them to do the same thing? If we are dealing with a younger child of three or four, we simply take the child by the hand, without interrupting the game or saying anything. When the game calls for gestures while standing in place, we have to make sure this child is standing close to us. In any case, it is advisable to always keep an eye on such children because they feel the special attention and that gives them something to hold onto internally. Generally, the child will forget about everything else and joyfully take part in the activity. There may be children who are not yet fully participating in the movements, at most walking along with the group. We simply let them be. However, we must always maintain our awareness of them. If, perhaps, a five-year-old causes a disturbance, or moves in an exaggerated, sloppy manner (for instance, stepping on another child's foot on purpose), we might pause for a moment, act surprised and say something like:

"Oh, it looks like you're wearing dirty shoes today. Come on, let's clean them up quickly."

We all pretend to brush our shoes and recite:

Brush, brush, clean the shoe,
Brush, brush, clean as new.

(Pretend to hold a shoe in your left hand and make the brushing motion with your right hand.)

Repeat the rhyme one time, followed by a gesture of putting on shoes, before continuing with the game. Or, maybe a shoe has lost its heel and, with an appropriate rhyme, has to be quickly nailed back on. Under certain circumstances, we just might meet a mother goose with her brood of newly hatched goslings that are only able to take tiny little steps. And so we are all walking with little goose steps. Naturally, we will have to think of a rhyme on the spur of the moment, or perhaps we will compose a couple of lines.

Sometimes, we might be surprised that a farmhand has let some seeds fall onto the path rather than in the field.

The important thing is that the children are distracted from foolish behavior by such small interruptions, as long as the "surprise" you are portraying seems real. If that does not work, I would also take those children

33

by the hand for a short time. If you say something like: "If you don't stop it right now, you can't play anymore," it is usually ineffective and does nothing to help create a happy atmosphere of play. If you are dealing with a six-year-old child who is not affected by an imaginative approach, it is perfectly fine to address the child directly. However, it is always better to tell a child what they should do, rather than what they should not do. Try to adhere to this pedagogical principle: never forbid anything without offering something else. For example, if a child is racing around the room as a flying bird, we could say:

"You're the mother bird who is flying very carefully."

Or, perhaps a snail is creeping along, but one child won't stop talking or making silly remarks:

"This isn't the time for talking; now the snail is taking a walk."

And if that does not help:

"And now you are very quiet."

This should be said firmly, but not loudly. Another option would be to take an older child to the side for a moment, without saying anything. It is important for these children to sense where the limits are. Such a response will make a child subconsciously feel that we really are standing by his or her side and providing support.

There are sometimes problems that arise that affect the group as a whole — when a new kindergarten teacher/group leader comes in who is perhaps not so familiar with leading rhythmic games in loosely formed groups, for example. It may create a sense of uncertainty. That person will need to look for a temporary solution until the children are well in hand. Children immediately sense any insecurity in an adult. It causes children to become easily distracted and unable to devote themselves fully to activities involving imitation.

There are certain days when we have to resort to special measures in order to guide the little flock into some kind of meaningful movement activity: on days when it is very windy outside, or a coming change in the weather that is clearly noticeable, or perhaps when a special event is going to take place, such as a circus. Such things tend to stimulate children to the point where they would rather roughhouse or jump all over the place. The following example is something that usually works like a charm:

"Today, Flippy Floppy Freddy is coming to visit." He is a fantasy character who does whimsical, playful things.

Flippy Floppy Freddy,
(With an index finger, tap your head)
Why are you unsteady?
(Tap your stomach)
I am not unsteady,
(Tap your back)
Just my name—Flippy Floppy Freddy!
(Tap your head)

Repeat the rhyme several times, with a different movement each time. For example:

Clap with your hands, or just two fingertips: in front, behind, above, front.

Tap with your toes: front, behind, to the side, feet together

Hop on one leg, the other leg, both feet, stand still.

This kind of harmless, frivolous activity immediately brings on a cheery mood in the children and, at the same time, has a calming, regulating effect. Suddenly, the children are attentively watching the adult, with expectant looks. You have to be sure to have enough ideas to keep their attention, which requires real internal effort. The verse should be very rhythmic, not too fast and spoken with small pauses. Naturally, Flippy Floppy Freddy's appearances must be few and far between, otherwise his effectiveness would be diminished. But every once in a while, a six- or seven-year-old, about to enter first grade, will try to test what happens if he simply refuses to participate in a circle game, for instance. If Flippy Floppy Freddy appears at this moment, the child will forget about testing the limits and fully participate in the game.

With increasing experience comes decreasing difficulties. It is a great help to the children if you work on developing your imagination and regularly make the effort to come up with new ideas.

In order for things to go smoothly with rhythmic games, it is necessary to give much thought to the activity that occurs beforehand and the transition into the following activity.

If the children have a bathroom time beforehand, afterward they could make their way to a table or a hallway (depending on your physical space). When the last child has arrived, you also sit at the table. Look around the table until your calm gaze has quieted the last foot-tapper and chatterbox. It requires only a momentary pause and you do not have to be pedantic about the children becoming completely quiet. Then you purposefully stand up and perhaps say something that has to do with the game: "Let's go get the scythes," if it is harvest sea-   35 son. Or simply, "Let's get to work."

Such a lively invitation almost always results in the children gladly following along. One thing to remember is that you should always begin with the activity immediately. You do not have to wait until the last child is in place or everyone is standing still; rather, immediately upon arrival, transition into the form of the movement that is to be imitated.

Of course, it is different if a morning song and verse are said before the rhythmic game activity. In that case, absolute quiet is necessary before you begin a song or verse.

At the end of the game we always do something to calm down, but it does not need to be longer than a few moments. For instance, if the game has involved a running horse, at the end it returns to the barn to rest. Or, perhaps the gnomes return from a hard day's work and fall asleep to a lullaby. Sometimes, you could say something like:

When the sun comes up and shines so bright,
Everyone awakens from a restful night,
And hurries to breakfast in the morning light.

Or, if the farmhands are returning from the fields, the farmer's wife stands at the door and says:

Come inside, if you please,
And dine on porridge and peas.

Or, after the game is ended, you might simply say: "Now it's snack time" or "Let's go eat snack now."

If another activity is to follow, you can simply come up with a similar kind of transition. In any case, it is a help to the children when you maintain a "good grip" on the transitions and have given them enough forethought. In this way, the rhythmic happenings are better able to resonate within the children, who will not then be so easily distracted and start acting out, requiring you to find some way to calm them down.

In the following section, some of the games, songs, rhymes, and dances already mentioned are presented in more detail and with suggestions for movements and gestures.

Songs, Verses, Games, and Dances for Circle Time

Rhythmic Games for Harvest Time

Note: A different version of the following circle can be found in *Dancing As We Sing*, edited by Nancy Foster (Acorn Hill/WECAN)

With happy stride and scythe in hand,
We go to mow the meadow land. REPEAT

Walk clockwise while shouldering the scythe.

Silvery scythes twinkling,
Golden sheaves sinking,
Spikey crowns, stems straight and tall,
The sun has ripened them all. (TITMANN)

Walk rhythmically while "mowing with the scythe."

We tie the sheaves,
We bind them tight,
We tie, we tie,
In the bright sunlight.

"Tie a bundle of stalks"; alternate lifting first the right arm and then the left.

We build a house of sheaves,
Where we can hide with ease, REPEAT
We swiftly slip right in,
And peek outside again.

Lift the sheaves with both hands and put in place.

Crouch down and indicate a peephole with the hands.

While sitting in the house of sheaves, we are sometimes surprised by a thunderstorm.
Say each line twice, knocking on the floor each time:

It's sprinkling … It's sprinkling … Gently tap index fingers together
It's raining … It's raining … Gently tap all the fingers together, one after the other
It's hailing … It's hailing … Knock finger knuckles together
It's rumbling … It's rumbling … Clap with palms on the floor
It's thundering … It's thundering … Drum with fists on the floor
It's lightning … It's lightning … Quickly dart in the air with both index fingers
The friendly sun is shining again. Form a sun with both arms

If it is a heavy thunderstorm, the movements become strong too; small storms go with gentle movements.

In the distance, we hear the farmer's wagon coming.

We load up the wagon with the golden crop,
REPEAT
And when we are done, we climb up on top.

A few "farmhands" stand to the side of the group "in the wagon" and catch the sheaves as they are tossed up. Everyone "jumps up."

Holding the reins with both hands, we walk and trot, taking the wagon back to the barn and singing:

Words: M. Garff; Melody: F. Jaffke

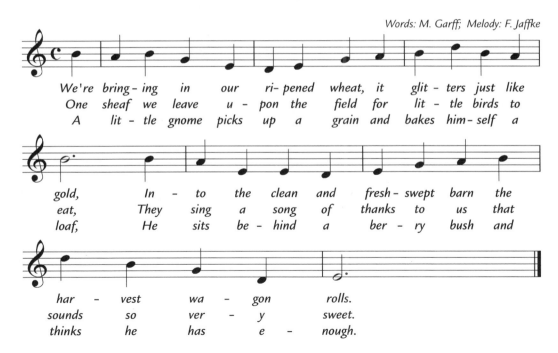

We're bring-ing in our ri-pened wheat, it glit-ters just like gold, In-to the clean and fresh-swept barn the har-vest wa-gon rolls.

One sheaf we leave u-pon the field for lit-tle birds to eat, They sing a song of thanks to us that sounds so ver-y sweet.

A lit-tle gnome picks up a grain and bakes him-self a loaf, He sits be-hind a ber-ry bush and thinks he has e-nough.

We jump down from the wagon.

With great delight we toss them down,
The golden sheaves upon the ground. REPEAT

The "farmhands" throw the sheaves down
and the others catch them.

We thresh, we thresh,
We thresh the grain,
And when it's done,
We start again.
The flails, they fly
To music's beat.
First I whack, then you whack,
Clip clop clap, clip clop clap. (FOLK VERSE)

Thresh with a threshing flail.

We gather the grain and put it in sacks, REPEAT

Form a semicircle in front of the body's midsection for
the sack. Fill the sack with the right hand. Tie the sack.

And carry it away upon our backs.
The heavy load won't dampen our will,
As we bring the grain to the miller to mill.

Shoulder the sacks and carry them while bent under
their weight.
Bring the sacks to the miller and ask him to mill the
flour.

Clip, clop, clap, millstones going 'round,
Bread aplenty once the flour's ground.

Lightly clap.

Blow a breeze, a friendly bluster,
Here atop our hill,
So the wings can turn the faster,
On our great windmill.

With outspread arms, carefully turn the windmill's
wings.

A waterwheel is also used to mill grain.

Grind, grind, grind so well,
Splash, splash, to the dell,
Day and night, waterwheel churns,
'Til the grain to flour is turned. (S. KÖNIG)

Slowly turn the hands around each other.

Now we bring the sack of flour to the baker.

The heavy load won't dampen our will,
As we bring the baker the flour from the mill.

Shoulder the sacks and carry them while bent under their weight.

The baker would like to make fruit pies for us, so he sends us to the garden to pick fruit.

Off to the garden, quick as we can,
Waiting here won't put pie in the pan. REPEAT

Walk around with a gesture of "holding a basket."

Little tree, quake,
Little tree, shake,

Stand in place, with arms forming an open circle, as if they are around a tree. Put weight on one foot, then the other while "shaking" the tree.

Throw the apples (or plums) down for me to take.

Show apples falling from the tree by moving hands and fingers as if it were "raining" apples.

We gather the apples (plums), every last one,
REPEAT
To take to the baker when we're done.

Pick up the apples with both hands and place them in the basket.
Carry the basket to the baker.

The baker will bake us a pie,
We all will get a piece to try.

Roll the dough, nice and thin,
Put it in the round pie tin.
REPEAT SEVERAL TIMES

We lay the fruit in the tin, layer after layer,
Room for some more right over there,
Maybe just one more...
And then we open the oven door.

Slide it, slide it, into the oven,
The pie will be done before eleven. REPEAT

Form a bowl with the left arm and stir clockwise with the other hand.

"Roll the dough," making large gestures with arms and hands.

Carefully lay the fruit pieces into the pie tin.

In a rhythmic motion, slide the pie into the oven.

There are several different ways to bring this game to a conclusion. You could let the tired farmhands and their assistants take a nap, falling asleep to a lullaby or sleeping song (sit and put your head on folded hands). Or, you could say something that would lead into the next activity — snack, for example.

The following is a song we sing when sharing the harvest bread at the harvest festival.

Song of the Bread

Words: M. Tittmann; Melody: F. Jaffke

1. From where, oh where does our good bread come? Do you not know? The ba-ker used flour to make us some, he knead-ed and formed the dough, and so the dough would rise a-lot, he baked it in an o-ven hot.

2. From where, oh where, does our flour come?
   Do you not know?
   The miller ground grain to make us some,
   With powerful millstones, heavy and slow,
   Grinding it stone on stone,
   The wind turns the windmill all alone.

3. From where, oh where, does our good grain come?
   Do you not know?
   The farmer used seeds to grow us some,
   The seeds that the farmer did sow,
   And in the field he seeded out,
   The little plants began to sprout.

4. From where, oh where, does the plants' life come?
   Do you not know?
   The Earth asked God to give them some.
   He blessed them with love and light to grow,
   The flowers he gave everyone,
   And wind and rain and dew and sun.

Giants and Gnomes

Little tunic swinging,

Little bell is ringing,
Little slippers slapping,
Two hands are clapping,
Little face peeking out,
Little gnome, no doubt! (M. GARFF)

Stand together in a loosely formed group. Using both hands, swish the tunic from side to side.
With hands raised slightly, ring a little bell in each hand.
Tap the floor with both feet.
Gently clap hands.
Hand to the forehead, in a searching gesture.
Point with an index finger raised in front of the chest or form a gnome's pointy cap.

Slip the magic tunic on,
Swirling magic mist,
So no one can spy upon
Our secret mountain tryst!
Grab hammer and tongs, don't be slow,
Stick them in a sack,
Put them on your back,
Now, it's off to the mountain we go!
Shoulder the sack and turn to go. (H. DIESTEL)

Grab the tunic with both hands, from front to back, two times.
Put both fists next to each other on the chest.

Hammer fists together, one on top of the other.

With sack on shoulder, take gnome steps clockwise around in a circle.

The gnomes, the gnomes
To the hills they roam,
Carry everything piggyback,
In a great big gnome knapsack.
Deep in a mountain, way down below,
A knocking, hammering little gnome. (S. RESKY)

Sit on the floor and hammer. Repeat several times; sometimes strongly, sometimes gently.

And here comes Old Giant, walking tall,
Looking defiant, big boots and all,
He's come to give the gnomes a fright,
They'll have to hide quite out of sight.
From out of their hidden gnome abode
They laugh at the mean old giant rogue.
If he comes back, perchance on a whim,
Whoosh! The gnomes disappear again. (ANON.)

Walk around taking heavy giant steps.

Quickly crouch down and hide head in arms.

"Laugh" with open hands and moving fingers.
Walk in giant steps.
Everyone quickly runs to a corner and sits.

There the giant's snoring,
Peacefully asleep.
On tiptoes we're going,
For a better peek.
We pluck at him here,
We poke at him there,
If he moves so near,
Whoosh! We disappear.

Point in the direction the giant is lying.

Walk toward the giant on tippy toes.

Cautiously poke at the "giant."

Wait for the giant to move.
Everyone runs back to the corner.

We tiptoe back to where the giant is sleeping
to see what he is doing now.

His mane, long uncombed,
The giant now shakes,
And stretches and groans,
Before he awakes.
Just for fun, someone tickles his nose,
With a feathery flit,
And the giant's nose blows,
"Aachoo!" in a sneezing fit. (M. GARFF)

Slowly stand up straight and gently shake your head.

Stretch with one arm and then the other.

Very gently stroke your nose with both hands.

Clap hands together on "Aachoo!"

The giant gets away from there,
And looks for another lair.

Walk around in giant steps.

Or:
The grumbling giant walked to the wood,
To find the rascal who'd tickled him good.

He sees the gnomes and asks:
"Did you do it?"

Look down like a giant.

We say:
"Certainly not."

Look up and shake your head "no."

So he turns around and goes home. REPEAT

Continue walking with heavy steps.

The gnomes quickly pick up their sacks and run for the mountains.

From the mountain, scurry, scurry,
Come the gnomes, hurry, hurry,
Carry silver sacks, run down the dell,

With sack on shoulders, run around on tiptoe.

Ringing, ringing, magic little bell:
Ting-a-ling-a-ling; ting-a-ling-a-ling...

Ring the little bell with one hand while standing.

In the mountain, scurry, scurry,
Hammering gnomes, hurry, hurry,
Gold and silver, run down the dell,

While sitting, hammer both fists together, or on the floor.

Ringing, ringing, magic little bell:
Ting-a-ling-a-ling; ting-a-ling-a-ling...

Ring the little bell with one hand.

48

In the mountain, scurry, scurry,
Tired gnomes to bed, hurry, hurry,
Sleep on soft pallets, dream of the dell,
Ringing, ringing, magic little bell:
Ting-a-ling-a-ling; ting-a-ling-a-ling... (H. DIESTEL)

Lay head on folded hands (sleeping gesture).

Very softly ring the little bell with one hand.

Evening wind, silky soft,
Tired hills, breeze aloft,
Sleepy peeps from little birds,
Sleepy gnomes — no sound heard.

While making the gesture for sleep, sit on the floor for the whole verse. You may also wish to sing the words to your own tune, or sing another sleeping song or lullaby.

Quickly find their little housey,
Down among the roots and loam,
Day's work's done and oh so drowsy,
Pirzel and Purzel, the little gnomes. (J. KLOSE)

You might also light lanterns for the "gnomes" to help them find their way home or to give light while they work. Give two children a little lantern that they may take turns holding. We sing one of the following two songs, or another lantern song.

Lantern Songs

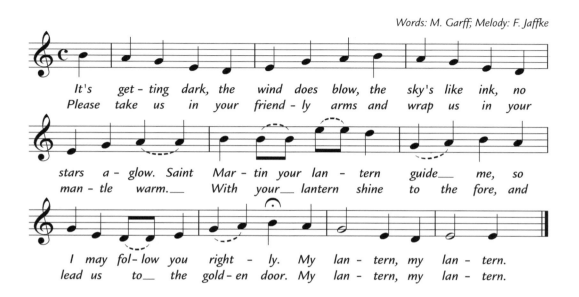

Words: M. Garff; Melody: F. Jaffke

It's get - ting dark, the wind does blow, the sky's like ink, no
Please take us in your friend - ly arms and wrap us in your

stars a - glow. Saint Mar - tin your lan - tern guide___ me, so
man - tle warm.___ With your___ lantern shine to the fore, and

I may fol - low you right - ly. My lan - tern, my lan - tern.
lead us to___ the gold - en door. My lan - tern, my lan - tern.

1. & 2. I go with my lit – tle lan – tern, and my lit-tle

lan-tern with me; A-bove,_ the stars_ are all_ a-glow, and

we_ shine down be-low. 1. So long burns my light, be-fore me so
2. If it____ goes out, no need_ to

bright, and it____ is with me all through the night
shout,____ we and our lan – terns turn – a – bout.

Where To, Where To, You Little Gnome?

Words: H. Diestel; Melody: I. Zickwolff

Where to, where to, you lit - tle gnome? Your sack is packed, where

do you roam? What glit - ters there so bold? I worked and forged a

lit - tle crown for Lit - tle Prince to wear a - round. It's

made from gleam - ing gold.

For this game, a group of children sits on the floor in the "gnome's workshop." A second group walks around while "shouldering the gnome sack" for the first six bars of the music. During the rest of the song, everyone hammers their fists together, one on top of the other, in time to the music. This is repeated several times, using a different golden object each time.

Examples of other objects (as suggested by N. Kuettel):
I worked and forged a necklace rare
to give to our good Queen to wear...
Or:
... a bracelet charm, for Princess to wear on her arm ...
... a little cup, the King will use it when he sups ...
... a finger ring, a very pretty little thing ...

Saint Nicholas

Words: M. Garff; Melody: A. Künstler

From heav'n-ly cas-tle heights, his steed a blaz-ing white, He's

ri-ding down to us, the ho-ly Saint Ni-cho-las.

2. Down in the wood, a hare
   Sniff-sniffs the frosty air,
   The elk with his big horns,
   Is bounding over bush and thorns.

3. And all dear creatures nigh,
   Come round and gaze up high,
   And bow down to his worth,
   St. Nicholas here on earth.

4. So we a song would sing,
   Of stars and silvery wings,
   That we'll not sing before
   He comes and knocks upon our door.

Verse 1: Two or three children play the role of Nicholas and walk around the rest of the loosely formed group with dignified steps. At the end they go to the middle of the group and stand there.

2: Together with the adults, all the other children move around "Nicholas" and indicate bunny ears with both hands on the head. Indicate elk horns by raising arms high and spreading fingers wide.

3: Indicate animal paws with your hands at chest height and walk in a circle. While standing, turn toward the middle and bow twice.

4: Walk around in a circle with arms crossed over your chest; then stand still, turned to the middle. "Knock on the door" with the right fist upon the open palm of the left hand.

Christmas Play

This little Christmas play, consisting of songs, poems and bridging texts, is not a traditional play with assigned roles and individual speaking parts. Everything is spoken or sung by adults together with the children, who put on a different costume each day and simply sing or speak along, more or less. Adults also perform all the walking, movements, and gestures with the children. Without being asked, there are always a few "angels" who will fold their hands and speak along with an adult when the shepherds are kneeling in front of the manger and praying to the Child, for example.

The play should take place completely within the context of imitation so that the children are able to become immersed in this wonderful event in a way that is appropriate for their age. It is not yet time for a play in which lines must be learned and each child is responsible for saying them individually.

This is an especially important consideration for parents when they are preparing for Christmas celebrations with their child's early childhood group. They should not hold to the notion that their children are going to perform something for them, but much more that they, as parents, are fellow players on this special day. Parents sit in a large semi-circle around us and quietly sing the songs with us. Some parents may accompany us musically on a lyre or a harp. Parents should not look steadily at their own child during the proceedings because it would interfere with the child's devotion to the activity.

Costumes and props

Mary: *Red dress or skirt and blue cloak*
Joseph: *Brown mantle, hat, walking stick, lantern*
Ox: *Brownish red cloth*
Donkey: *Blue cloth*
Angel: *Yellow or white tunic and a fine yellow cloth used as a veil held in place by a crown-band*
Angel that carries the star: *Yellow or white tunic, crown-band with five-pointed star, a rod with a six-pointed star on one end*
Shepherds: *Colorful cotton cloths tied as cloaks, or simple tunics; hats*
Gifts: *As many gifts as needed for all the shepherds to have something to bring to the manger; these may include wool fleece, "bottles" for milk made out of birch bark, and sheepskins to represent lambs.*

Sequence of action

The first thing is to arrange the chairs, manger and gifts table (see illustration) and lay out the costumes. After each child is in costume, he or she sits in an assigned place. As soon as all the children are in their costumes, make sure the "star-angel" has the rod and star, one angel has the "Child" to carry and Joseph has his walking stick and lantern. Then all the angels stand and go to the "Angel House." They stand so that the "star-angel" is in front. The other angels are behind the "star-angel," with the one carrying the Child the very last in the row. Mary and an accompanying angel stand in front of the "star-angel." Joseph, the ox and the donkey go to their shelter (see illustration) and the shepherds remain seated.

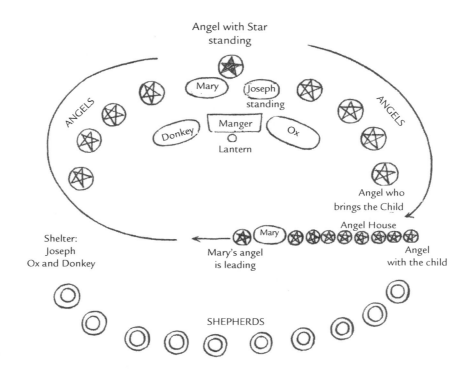

56

With arms crossed over her chest and led by an angel, Mary walks around the semicircle, accompanied by the song below. After the second verse of the song is complete, all the angels join Mary and walk with her. When the song is ended, the angels return to their places and sit. The angel with the Child remains standing by the chair. The angel carrying the star stands behind Mary.

Words: K. Schubert; Melody: F. Jaffke

O - ver all the shin - ing heav - ens goes__ Ma - ri - a
Ma - ry's jour - ney, each__ step pre - cious, Choir of stars__ sees
Sun__ is bu - sy with__ the weav - ing, spark - ling light__ for
Sun__ and Moon joined all__ the stars___ in__ their great__ train

qui - et - ly. Bliss - ful gold - en light___ she
ev' - ry one, 'Tis__ her hon - or to__ pre -
Ba - by's gown; Ask__ the Moon to please__ be
up a - bove, Sing - ing songs from worlds__ a -

gath - ers for__ the Child___ who is to be.
pare us for__ the Christ - mas that is to come.
giv - ing so__ the Child___ in joy a - bounds.
far, and bear - ing to Earth___ this gift of love.

57

Joseph sets down the lantern for light,
Inside the stable it has to be bright.

Joseph places the lantern in front of the manger and then goes to stand next to Mary.

Holding up their little paw-hands, the donkey and then the ox walk around behind the semicircle of angels to the following song, and come to stand by the manger.

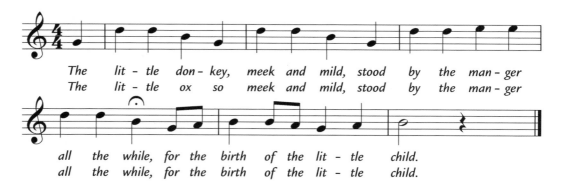

The lit-tle don-key, meek and mild, stood by the man-ger
The lit-tle ox so meek and mild, stood by the man-ger

all the while, for the birth of the lit-tle child.
all the while, for the birth of the lit-tle child.

The angel carrying the "Child" now walks to the manger and puts the baby into Mary's arms; then the angel returns to her chair.

Sing "Joseph Dearest, Joseph Mine." Mary rocks the baby in her arms. Joseph, all the angels and the shepherds also make a gesture with their arms to indicate rocking a baby.

At the end of the song, Mary lays the baby in the manger.

Traditional German carol; Oxford Book of Carols, #77 (verses 1 & 2, without refrain)

Jo- seph, dear est, Jo- seph mine, Help me cra- dle the child di - vine,
Glad - ly, dear one, la - dy mine, Help I cra- dle this child of thine;

God re - ward thee and all that's thine In
God's own light on us both shall shine In

Par - a - dise, so prays the mo - ther Ma - ry.
Par - a - dise, as prays the mo - ther Ma - ry.

The shepherds stand and walk around the semicircle of angels to the next song.

During the second verse of the song, the shepherds remain standing in a loosely formed group by their chairs and move their fingers to indicate they are playing the wooden flute. During the third verse, they sit down in their chairs and make a gesture to indicate they are sleeping.

Melody: F. Jaffke

What to do, the shep - herd asks? So they will all
Woo - den flute now comes to mind, Bell - like tones with
That's why no lambs walk a - lone, Stay here near the

stay and rest, He with all those lit - tle lambs,
sound sub - lime, Sweet - ly play - ing for the lambs,
shep - herd's song. With the shep - herd stay at home,

So they will all stay and rest.
Bell - like tones with sound sub - lime.
Stay here near the shep - herd's song.

While singing the next song, the angels stand and walk to the shepherds with arms crossed over their chest. An adult takes the lead, then the angel with the star and the rest of the angels.

Traditional German carol; Oxford Book of Carols #118 (verse 3)

It fell___ u - pon the high___ mid night. Ei - a, ei -

a, Su - san - ni, su - san - ni, su - san - ni. The stars they

shone both fair___ and bright, Al - le - lu - ia, al - le - lu -

ia. The an - gels sang___ with all their might.

61

The angels remain standing close together in a semicircle behind the shepherds during the next song.

On the second verse, the angels open their arms in a gesture of announcing news.

Traditional hymn by Martin Luther; Words translated by Catherine Winkworth

From heav'n a - bove to earth I come To bear good news to__
To you this night is born a child Of Ma - ry, cho - sen__

ev - ery home; Glad ti - dings of____ great
mo - ther mild; This lit - tle child____ of

joy__ I bring, Where - of I will now__ say__ and sing.
low__ ly birth Shall be the joy of__ all__ your earth.

While humming the melody once more, the angels go back to their places, walking with arms crossed in front of their chests.

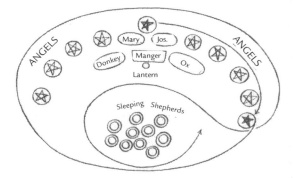

Oh___ what is this___ won-der that our eyes now be -
Ga-ther in close, ga-ther in close, the___ sheep come a -

hold? Though the hour is but mid-night, see the dawn's rays of___
run-ning. Ga-ther in close, gather in close, and___ I'll tell you___

gold.___ Look, a___ won-der here, Look, a___ won-der here. The___
some thing. In the___ sta-ble there, In the___ sta-ble there, Look, a

stars are bla-zing bright,___ Light-ing up_____ the night.
won-der, look, a won-der, gath-er in___ close right here.

During the above song, the shepherds awaken, stand up and are amazed. Softly clap on "dawn's rays." On "Look, a wonder here," put hands to the forehead to indicate gazing far away. On "stars are blazing bright," draw a big circle in the air with your arms.

During the second verse, the shepherds walk, rubbing sleep from their eyes, around the semicircle of angels to the gift table.

63

SPOKEN:

Now we should think and wonder and muse,
What is it the precious Child could use?
I will give Him wool, fine and thick,
His mother can gently lay Him on it.
A bottle of milk will make a good soup,
His mother can cook it outside on the stoop.
I'll bring Him a lamb, full of joy,
A lovely playmate for the Boy.

The shepherds remain by the gift table and form a bowl with their hands.

As the gifts are spoken of, an adult hands them to two or three children, depending on how many gifts there are.

Then, during the following song the shepherds happily walk around the angels once more and then go stand across from the "Angel House." They carry the gifts with both hands.

Traditional German carol

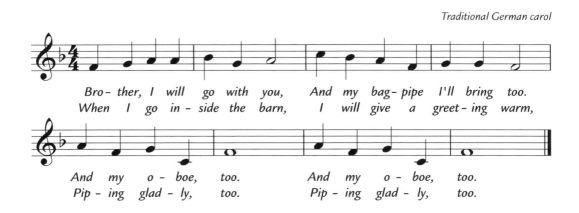

Bro- ther, I will go with you, And my bag- pipe I'll bring too.
When I go in - side the barn, I will give a greet- ing warm,

And my o - boe, too. And my o - boe, too.
Pip - ing glad - ly, too. Pip - ing glad - ly, too.

The shepherds make a knocking gesture during the following song while holding the gifts in one hand.

After the first verse, they wait until Joseph arrives.

During the second verse Joseph waves the shepherds inside and points to the manger. Then he returns to his place.

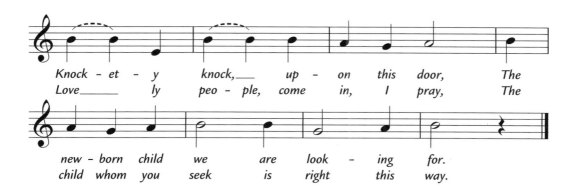

Greetings to you, oh Child so dear,
I'm so glad that we found you here.
I bring you some wool, fine and thick,
So your mother can lay you on it.

This bottle of milk will make a good soup,
Your mother can cook it outside on the stoop.
And I bring you a lamb, full of joy,
A lovely playmate for a boy.

SPOKEN PRAYER:

Rockabye, rockabye, holy night,
Angels have brought a child of light.
All people shall bless Him,
All creatures caress Him,
All flowers He will gladly greet,
All stones will worship at His feet,
All beings will serve Him,
Cherubim and Seraphim. (HERBERT HAHN)

The shepherds cautiously walk to the manger and
stand in front of it in a semicircle.
The shepherds carrying the wool step forward and give
it to Mary and step back again. Mary puts the wool in
the manger.
The shepherds hand Mary the "milk."

The shepherds place their "lambs" on the floor in front
of the manger.

All the shepherds kneel, take off their hats and put
them on the floor in front of them. Then they fold
their hands to pray.

During the following song, everyone "rocks the baby"
in their arms.

66

Words from the Tyrol region of Germany; Melody: A. Künstler

Wind, be still, be still, I say! Don't dis-turb His sleep to-day.

No more gales, and no more gusts, He's just closed his eyes to rest.

Wind, he's sleep-ing, the One who says When to storm in

surg - ing waves, or when to hush and

be so still, As He will, as He will.

67

Dear shepherds all, we thank you from our heart,
For your kind gifts and loving regard.

Joseph and Mary say their thanks, but, of course, everyone may say it with them.

The shepherds stand up, take their hats and bow towards the Child.

The shepherds turn from the manger and speak among themselves.

Let us joyfully run to our brothers,
And bring the good news to all the others.

During the final song, the shepherds walk around once again and return to their places.

Traditional German carol; from the Shorter New Oxford Book of Carols, #99

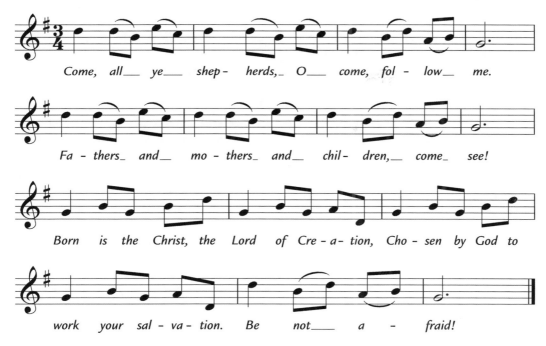

Come, all___ ye___ shep - herds,_ O___ come, fol - low_ me.

Fa - thers_ and_ mo - thers_ and_ chil - dren,__ come_ see!

Born is the Christ, the Lord of Cre - a- tion, Cho - sen by God to

work your sal - va - tion. Be not___ a - fraid!

After a few moments for reflection, the "donkey," or another child, blows out the light in the lantern.

To make sure there is a smooth transition and the children do not become chaotic, an adult should take the rod and star and Joseph's walking stick and put them away while changing out of their costumes immediately. Then the hats are gathered and the little ones are helped with fastenings on their costumes and everything is neatly folded.

Three Kings Play

This play, adapted by Freya Jaffke from a story by E. Proske, is structured as a story that is interspersed with songs and poems. To begin the play, the children sit in a large circle, in costume. An adult tells the story and sings—without demanding participation with the singing and speaking—and also leads the way for the angels and kings.

Costumes and props

Mary: *Red dress, blue cloak; gesture of carrying child in her arms*

Joseph: *Brown or purple mantle, walking stick*

Angel with Star: *Yellow or white long dress, crown with five-pointed star, rod with five-pointed star or a star with a picture of Mary and the Child on it*

Angel: *Yellow or white dresses or pieces of cloth to wrap around, crown with five-pointed star*

Red King: *Red mantle or cape, gold or red crown*

Blue King: *Blue mantle or cape, gold or blue crown*

Green King: *Green mantle or cape, gold or green crown*

Pages:

    Red – *Red cloth, gold circlet*

    Blue – *Blue cloth, gold circlet*

    Green – *Green cloth, gold circlet*

On a little table to the side, three different gift offerings are ready for the Kings. Instead of a manger, there is a small stool covered in blue cloth with a large candle placed on top.

The story

When the Child was born in Bethlehem, a star appeared in the sky that was more golden and brilliant than anyone had ever seen before. And if you looked closely at the star, you could see an image of the Holy Mother and her Child.

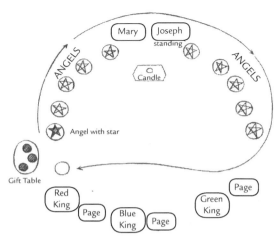

Led by an angel carrying a star, the other angels walk around before stopping in a large semicircle in front of the kings.

The song below is repeated until everyone has arrived at their place:

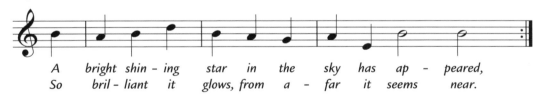

A bright shin - ing star in the sky has ap - peared,
So bril - liant it glows, from a - far it seems near.

The angels open their arms in a gesture of proclamation and sing while standing:

Toward Beth - le - hem far the star is guid - ing,
As if it is there we should be rid - ing.

While the first song, "A Bright Shining Star," is sung again, the angels return to their places.

In the East, there lived three kings: The Red King, the Blue King and the Green King. They were wise and pious men.

The Red King had a high tower. At night, he would climb to the top of the tower so he could gaze at the stars. And one night, he saw the star with the image of the Mother and her Child. He wanted to follow that star. KING SPEAKS:

The Red King stands up.

> *Page, bring me the gold, with its rosy glow,*
> *A fine gift it will make for the Child, you know.*

The Red Page fetches the gift from the table and gives it to the Red King.

The Blue King had a great hall in his castle. At night, he would open the massive doors of the hall so the stars could shine in. And one night, he saw the star with the image of the Mother and her Child. He wanted to follow that star. KING SPEAKS:

The Blue King stands up.

> *Page, bring me the frankincense, sweet and pure,*
> *A fine gift it will make for the Child, that's sure.*

The Blue Page fetches the gift from the table and gives it to the Blue King.

The Green King had a large chamber dug out from the earth. At night, he would sit in it and gaze up at the light of the stars. And one night, he saw the star with the image of the Mother and her Child. He wanted to follow that star. KING SPEAKS:

73

Page, bring me the myrrh, with its precious scent,
A fine gift it will make for the Child Heaven sent.

The Kings had to travel very far. The night was dark
and they did not know the way.

Then the Star appeared and guided them.

The Green King stands up:

The Green Page fetches the gift from the table and
gives it to the Green King.
The Kings remain standing.

The angel with the star steps in front of the Red King.
During the song below, the Kings and Pages walk once
around. The angel with the star then goes to stand
behind Mary, and the Kings stand in a semicircle a
little distance in front of the candle.

F. Jaffke

The three kings are trav - el - ing day by day, to
Beth - le - hem; guid - ing star leads the way.

The Star stopped moving over the small town of
Bethlehem. Being very watchful, the Kings entered
the town and asked about the little Child.

The Kings and Pages go near to the candle and stand
around it in a semicircle.

Mary greets them, but everyone may sing along:

74

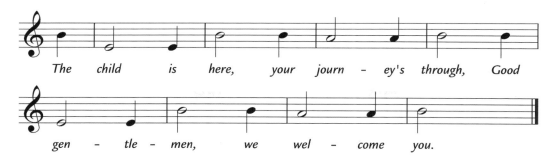

The child is here, your journ - ey's through, Good
gen - tle - men, we wel - come you.

SPOKEN:

The Star has led us to you,
Oh King, to Whom all praise is due.

The Kings and Pages kneel down and place their gifts around the candle, one after the other, to the following text:

What's brightening this night with darkness fraught?
It's gold that Melchior for the child has brought.

The Red King sets down his gift.

What's wafting toward us in tendrils of silver?
It's the fine frankincense that Balthazar delivers.

The Blue King sets down his gift.

What's perfuming the air, a healing herb?
It's the scent of Caspar's gift of myrrh.

The Green King sets down his gift.

Gold, incense, and myrrh; heart, will, and mind,
For the child of God's mercy they have fared far to
    find. (M. GARFF)

The Kings and Pages stand up again.

Kings of the East, wise and calm,
May our gratitude soothe like balm.
May God protect you on your way,
May He bless you every day.

Mary and Joseph say their thanks, but everyone may say it along with them.

The Kings and Pages bow in farewell. Led by the angel
with the star, they return to their places.

F. Jaffke

The three kings are jour-ney-ing east-ward home, through
de-serts to-ward the sun they roam.

During the first two lines of the following verse, the
angels stand up quietly and form a circle.

In the dark deep night, when all eyes were closed,
An angel appeared while Joseph dozed:
"Joseph, Joseph, wake up, dear man,
And make your way to Egypt land,
Take the Child and his mother, too,
The path will be clear; God is with you."

The angels then quietly return to their seats.

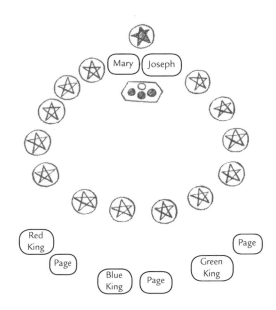

76

Joseph takes Mary by the hand,
And goes with her to Egypt land.

Mary stands up and steps with Joseph in front of the table with the candle. During the following song, they walk around the outside once until they come to the narrator.

Fare - well, fare - well, our jour - ney we must start, Fare -

well, fare - well, for E - gypt we de - part.

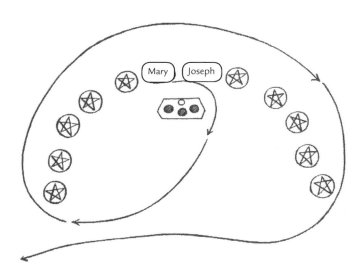

Before the children take off their costumes, one child will put out the candle with a snuffer.

In Winter

For the song below, everyone walks around
in a loosely formed circle, clockwise, while
gesturing to indicate snowflakes falling.

E. Proske

Snow, snow, snow - white flakes fall from hea - ven to the lake;

Here's a fril - ly bon - net with la - cy snow flowers on it;

And the sleds they slide a - way, on the hill where dwarfs do play.

Snow, snow, snow - white flakes fall from hea - ven to the lake.

It's snowing, it's blowing,
A bitter, biting, blast,
Birds hide in the hazelnut bush,
And children run so fast.

Even the sparrows in the hazelnut bush are
covered in snow:

In winter-bare hazelnut shrubbery
Sit three sparrows, belly to belly.

Sit or stand in a loosely formed group. Using both hands, indicate the bushes, drawing a large arc in the air. Place both fists together on the chest.

Eric on the right; on the left, Frank,
And right in the middle, cheeky Hank.

Using both hands, indicate the right, left and middle.

They all have their eyes closed very tight,
Up above it's snowing with all its might!

Put hands over eyes.
Indicate snow by gesturing with both hands.

They squish close together, no room for a draft,
Snugger than snug was our Hank, fore and aft.

Put fists together on the chest and hunch up a little.

The three could hear their heartbeats, drumming
    away.

Drum the right index finger on the left palm.

And if they've not gone, they're still there today.

Folded hands.

(C. MORGENSTERN)

This poem may be repeated several times.

Before we hitch up the horse to the sleigh, we put new shoes on the horse to the following song. We choose three verses and use three different types of hammering, one for each verse: normal, very gentle and very strong, by knocking our fists together, one on top of the other.

The Blacksmith

Your hooves I shoe, stay good and true, Fine
When mas - ter rides, stars are your guides, Your
Up - hill, down - hill, o'er beck and rill, Light
On ev' - ry ride, up - hill you glide, Your
Your hooves I shoe, stay good and true, Now

lit - tle horse, come back, of course!
way is clear when star - light's near!
as the air through val - leys fair!
rid - er tries to touch the sky!
lit - tle horse, come back, of course!

Now we hitch the little horse to the sleigh:

To the sleigh that's big and broad,
My nickering horse I hitch.
When I'm done I must applaud,
Horse trots at a fever pitch.

"Hold the horse's reins" in both hands while standing.

Up the hill, down the other side,
Mother Sun is shining bright;
We travel the land, far and wide,
Villages covered by snow so white.

"Holding the reins," trot around in a circle clockwise.

Just listen, the bells are ringing,
The wind is whistling by;
Little horse, joyfully running,
Have to hold the reins tight.

Using the same gesture as above, walk around the circle rhythmically.

Little horse, no longer running,
Is tuckered out from the ride;
In the distance, bells are ringing,
Softly ringing, eventide. (F. JAFFKE)

While standing: arms outstretched downward, fingertips touching, "swing the heavy bell."

At the Fishing Pond

A circle game by Suse König; Melody: F. Jaffke

Friend Pe-ter went a-fish-ing with his long and slen-der pole, He
Hey, Gre-tel, I know what to do, we'll walk out on the shore, We'll

threw his line in-to the lake, that line no fish did take. They
take a-long a lit-tle net, and man-y fish we'll get. They

wig-gled and gig-gled and had a grand old time, They
splished___ and splashed_____ and said, O let us out! They

wig-gled and gig-gled and had a grand old time.
splished___ and splashed__ and said, O let us out!

Dear-est Han-sel, what now?__ Dear-est Gre-tel, look at me! I'll__

count how man-y but-tons on your jack-et I see.

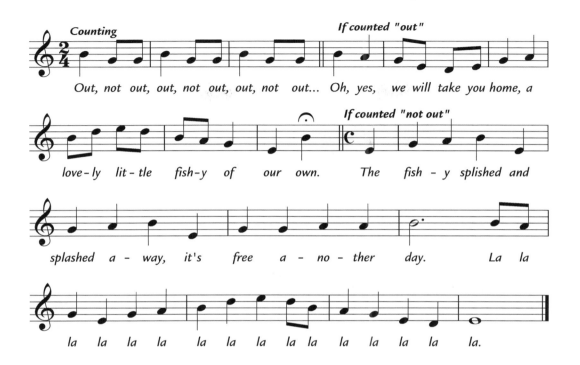

Counting

If counted "out"

Out, not out, out, not out, out, not out... Oh, yes, we will take you home, a

If counted "not out"

love-ly lit-tle fish-y of our own. The fish-y splished and

splashed a-way, it's free a-no-ther day. La la

la la la la la la la la la la la la la.

For this game, the first thing is to form a circle with the children. One third of the children will be the fish and sit in the middle of the circle. The children standing in the circle are paired up so they will know who their partner is when it is time to "make a net."

See page 85 for further instructions.

At the Fishing Pond – Instructions

First repeat:

Bars 1-4: Walk clockwise in a circle, holding hands.

Bars 5-8: While standing, do a gesture to indicate throwing a fishing line into the water.

Bars 9-12: The children in the middle "swim" around like fish, laughing by moving their fingers; then sit down in the middle again.

Second repeat:

Bars 1-4: Walk clockwise in a circle again, holding hands.

Bars 5-8: The children standing form a "net" with their partner. On "whoosh" all the "little fish" from the middle of the circle "swim" into a net and are caught; one "fish" per "net."

Bars 9-12: The child in the net moves both hands to indicate a swimming fish.

Ending:

Bars 13-20: Everyone gently claps, including the children with the net.

Bar 21ff.: Out, not out, out, not out, etc.: Count the number of buttons on a child's shirt or jacket.

If the counting lands on "not out": The "net and fish" step out of the circle. At the end we say: "One, two, three, all little fish are free," and let them "swim" back to the middle.

If the counting lands on "out": The "fish" swim back to the middle until the song is ended. The other children remain standing.

85

Cobbler Leatherfine

We go to Cobbler Leatherfine,
Any size shoe at any time.
Walk around in a circle with normal steps.

Will you walk with a giant's steps?
Walk around with large steps.

Giant shoes are what you should get:
Giant's stride — shoes long and wide.

Will you walk with a gnome's small steps?
Walk around with tiny steps.

Little shoes are what you should get:
Gnome's pace — short shoes win the race,
It's customary at every gnome place.

We have arrived at the cobbler's workshop.

I am the cobbler Leatherfine,
Any size shoe at any time.
While sitting, hammer fists together, one on top of the other.

I cut out the finest leather,
Sew new shoes for all kinds of weather.
Hold left hand flat with palm up to indicate the leather. With right hand (middle and index fingers) make a scissor movement to indicate cutting the leather.

Sewing, sewing, pull the needle through; REPEAT
Hold the "leather" in the left hand. "Sew" the leather with the right hand.

I hammer the hobnails sure and fast,
Soon I'll be done and these shoes will last.
"Hammer" fists together.

Now we will make the second shoe.
Repeat the text: "I am the cobbler Leatherfine..."

Cobbler Leatherfine, dearest man,
Thank you for these shoes made by hand.
I will put them on right away,
So I can joyfully dance (or hike) today.

Sometimes we also clean the shoes:

Brush, brush, clean the shoe,
Brush, brush, clean as new. REPEAT

Stand up and bow in gratitude.

Put on the "shoes."

Put left hand inside the "shoe" to hold it and "brush" the shoe with the right hand.

The Merry Tradespeople

Melody: F. Jaffke

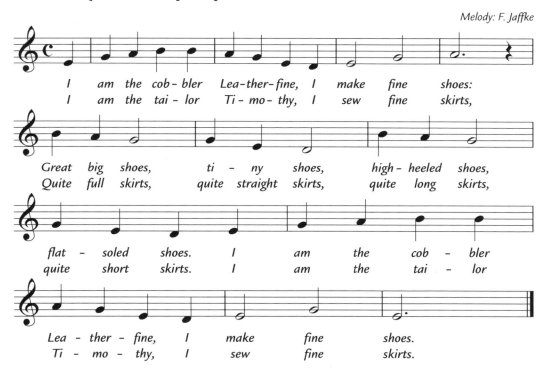

I am the cob - bler Lea-ther-fine, I make fine shoes:
I am the tai - lor Ti - mo - thy, I sew fine skirts,

Great big shoes, ti - ny shoes, high-heeled shoes,
Quite full skirts, quite straight skirts, quite long skirts,

flat - soled shoes. I am the cob - bler
quite short skirts. I am the tai - lor

Lea - ther - fine, I make fine shoes.
Ti - mo - thy, I sew fine skirts.

3. *I am the good cook Catherine, I cook fine soup:*
   So much soup, a little soup, very sweet soup,
      sour soup.
   I am the good cook Catherine, I cook fine soup.

4. *I am the joiner Jeremy, I make fine stools:*
   Great big stools, little stools, high-up stools,
      down-low stools.
   I am the joiner Jeremy, I make fine stools.

5. *I am the baker Pretzelgood, I bake good bread:*
   Great big loaves, little loaves, long loaves, short
      loaves.
   I am the baker Pretzelgood, I bake good bread.

6. *I am the painter Brushinhand, I paint fine walls:*
   Great big walls, little walls, long walls, short
      walls.
   I am the painter Brushinhand, I paint fine walls.

7. *I am the fisher Catchalot, I catch fine fish:*
   Quite big fish, quite small fish, quite fat fish,
      quite thin fish.
   I am the fisher Catchalot, I catch fine fish.

8. *I am the little Springinfield, I jump so well:*
   Quite big jumps, quite small jumps, quite long
      jumps, quite short jumps.
   I am the little Springinfield, I jump so well.

With each verse, a different small group of children goes to the middle of the circle and does the movements that go with that verse. Naturally, all the other children do the movements along with them. For the last verse, "little Springinfield," everyone jumps around clockwise in a loosely formed group.

The Wash-Women

Melody: F. Jaffke

Oh show me your feet, now, and show me your shoes, Look close-ly and see what the wash-wo-men do: They wash-wash, they wash-wash, the whole day long, They wash-wash, they wash-wash, the whole day long.

Subsequent verses follow the same pattern:

... They wring-wring, they wring-wring, the whole day long.
They wring-wring, they wring-wring, the whole day long.
... They hang clothes, they hang clothes ...
... They iron, they iron ...
... They fold clothes, they fold clothes ...
... Dance merrily, dance merrily ...

On bars 1 – 4: Extend the right foot and tap toes two times on the floor; switch feet and do the same thing.
On bars 5 – 8: Do the movements that correspond with each line of text.

Note: Two different versions of this song can be found as "The Washerwomen" in *Merrily We Sing* by Ilian Willwerth, and *The Singing, Playing Kindergarten* by Daniel Udo De Haes (both WECAN).

Knack the Gnome

Knack the Gnome pulled a bulb
From the woods where he went a lot,
And for the special spring celebration,
A little blue blossom bloomed on top.

Sit on the floor in a loosely formed group. With both hands make the form of a flower bud that slowly opens into a flower.

Knack the Gnome hollered to the hare,
Hidden in its hidey hole hamlet:
"Run, run, tell everyone there,
Blooming is my little blue violet."

Gesture with the right arm to call the hare.

Make bunny ears with hands on head and listen.

And the swallows swiftly soaring,
And the eagle eyeing from its eyrie,
And the mole mulling in the moor,
Rushing down the dell, the deer:

"Fly around" with outspread arms.
With hands to forehead look down in a searching gesture.
With hands below the chin, "dig" like a mole.
Rhythmically and lightly skip.
(These lines should always be repeated so the gestures do not change too quickly for the children.)

All drew near, hooved, furred, and plumed,
Bowed down with their best attention
To see the little blue flower that bloomed
For the spring celebration.

Stand still. Lean slightly forward and put hands to forehead in a searching gesture.
With both hands make the form of a flower bud that slowly opens.

(From *Rhythmen und Reime*; see Bibliography)

Note: Another version of this poem can be found as "Drake the Dwarf" in *The Seasonal Festivals in Early Childhood*, ed. Nancy Foster (WECAN).

If you have mostly five- and six-year-olds, you could try having two to four children play each character: swallows, mole, etc. They sit in a corner and the hare (also two to four children) comes to get them one by one. They wait by the Gnome until all are gathered. The last four lines of the poem are done all together again.

The Easter Bunnies

Sit on the floor in a loosely formed group.
Use hands to indicate bunny ears.

Mother Rabbit waits in the woods,
Her little bunnies return when they should.

"Hold an egg" in the left hand. Dip the "brush" in the
"paint" with the right hand and "paint the egg."

Today we will paint the eggs by hand;
Everyone do the best job you can.
We gently dip our brush in the paint,
And every egg gets a golden tint.

Carefully stand up, walk around and gently put the egg
in any corner of the room.

In secret corners, not too wide,
Eagerly the eggs we hide;
Upon a straw nest,
A golden egg rests,
And Easter Bunnies hop by so fast.

Hop back to the middle.

Now the children hunt for the eggs.

Walk around with careful steps.

Under trees of birch
We will search,
Under trees of linden
We will find them,
Upon a straw nest,
A golden egg rests,
Bring them all to Mother so fast.

Pick up the found "egg" and put it in the big basket
that an adult indicates with her arms at the end.

Go through the whole poem at least two times, changing the color of the eggs; red, blue, silver, etc. The
children who are hunting eggs should always return to
the same place they were before, as the Easter Bunny
hiding eggs.

Planting the Garden

The milkmaids and the farmer's wife
Get no rest until they're done.
So many things in a farmer's life,
Planting the garden is one.

Walk around clockwise, carrying a hoe on your shoulder.

We till the soil, arms so stout,
So all the little seeds can sprout,
We weed and weed until we stop,
Then onto the grass we flop.

"Till the soil" in a rhythmic motion.

Now we rest, strength is sapped,
So we curl up for a nap.

Sit on the floor.

Flying down so silently,
Mrs. Twitterling, the chickadee —
She needs refreshment for her tum,
Pecks at the ground, looks for a crumb.

Several children play the chickadee. They "fly" around with outspread arms, pecking "little crumbs" from the outstretched hands of the other children.

We'll give you a crumb, have no fear,
And a kernel of grain from an ear.
Up flies cheery chickadee, happy little thing,
Good-bye, good-bye, Mrs. Twitterling. (F. JAFFKE)

"The chickadees" fly away on the outside of the circle. The children on the floor wave good-bye.

Everyone stands up and makes a gesture of a bowl with the hands. Now the farmer's wife (an adult) will divide up the seeds among the children, saying the name of the seeds while doing so.

Into your little bowls I lay
All the seeds you'll need today.

We sow the seeds, seeds so small,
Spreading, scattering, one and all,
Upon them soft earth we sprinkle,
Then they sleep for a winkle.

Soon the tiniest tip of a sprout,
Pops up through a crack and looks about,
The little plants start to grow,
So we water them, you know,
And when we wait nice and patiently,
Bluebells in the garden we soon will see. (H. DIESTEL)

Little fairies who bring the rain,
Carry it in a watering can,
They water the leeks, they water the thyme,
They water the asters and columbines.
And when the water can flow no more,
Then there's no more rain in store. (M. GARFF)

Raining, raining, drop by drop,
Raining drops on my top knot,
Dropped from buckets in the clouds,
All the flowers' heads are bowed,
All the flowers show their love,
For the drink from sky above. (GERMAN FOLK VERSE)

The adult makes the gesture of distribuing seeds to the children. The verse is sung to the pentatonic scale.

Sit on the floor. We hold the "seeds" in the left hand and "seed them out" with the right.
Make a gesture of covering the seeds with both hands.

With folded hands, form the tip of a sprout and let it slowly grow upwards.
Open hands slightly.

Both hands open like a flower blooming.
The last line could be varied according to the kind of seeds that are handed out (for instance, "Thyme in the garden…" or "Sunflowers in the garden…").

Either while sitting or walking, wiggle fingers of both hands in a gesture of rain falling.

The following verse is also suitable:

96

The House with Five Chambers

Words: Stilke/Jaffke; Melody: F. Jaffke

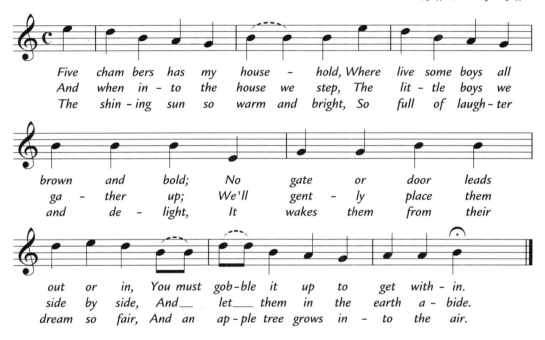

Five cham bers has my house — hold, Where live some boys all
And when in - to the house we step, The lit - tle boys we
The shin - ing sun so warm and bright, So full of laugh - ter

brown and bold; No gate or door leads
ga - ther up; We'll gent - ly place them
and de - light, It wakes them from their

out or in, You must gob - ble it up to get with - in.
side by side, And__ let__ them in the earth a - bide.
dream so fair, And an ap - ple tree grows in - to the air.

In the middle of a circle sit several children who are the "little boys."

Verse 1: Walk around in a circle, holding hands.

Verse 2: One of the older children in the circle goes to the middle, takes the "boys" by the hand and leads them once around the circle.

The "boys" sit down in the middle of the circle again and hide their head in their folded arms.

Verse 3: Two or three children are the "sun" and they walk around the "boys." The "boys" slowly stretch out their arms to indicate tree branches.

Fairy Dance

On misty, foggy evenings,
Silky, secret whisperings,
Cracking, creaking, clanking, clinking,
Soles so soft, slipping, slinking.

Walk around as noiselessly as possible.

Tappingman and Spinningfine,

On "Tapppingman" indicate a pointy cap on your head. On "Spinningfine" hold up the index finger.

Dancing on a circle line,
Light the candle wick,

With arms in the air, turn around once in a circle. Surround the index finger (candle) with the other hand to protect the "flame."

Whoosh — they're gone so quick. (M. GARFF)

On "Whoosh" clap softly and then sit down on the floor.

Fairy child in snail's snug house,
Hidden like a little mouse.
Comes along a ladybug,
Gives her a good morning hug,
Takes the fairy by the hand,
Flies with her throughout the land.

Half of the group sits on the floor (not too close together) as fairy children. The rest walk once around the circle. Each child stops in front of a "fairy child," takes her hand and "flies" around the circle clockwise.

Wicker, wacker, snicker, snacker,
Knot's just getting tighter,
Fairy child in snail's snug house,
Hidden like a little mouse.

Comes along a ladybug,
Gives her a good morning hug,
Takes the fairy by the hand,
Flies with her throughout the land.

Kitten's mittens, kitten's paws
Undo the knot without your claws.

If the group has enough five and six-year-olds, you will be able to walk in a spiral that gets tighter as you go. The children hold hands and are led by an adult. The text is repeated until the spiral is wound about 1½ times. Then one child sits in the middle as the "fairy child."

One child comes as the "ladybug" (index fingers pointing out from forehead to indicate feelers) into the snail spiral, bows to the fairy child, takes her by the hand, "flies" out with her and stands at the end of the spiral. Repeat the text several times as needed.

You could also say this verse to unwind the spiral. Repeat as many times as necessary until the snail spiral is unwound.

The Firefly

German Folk Song

A fie - ry fai - ry's fly - ing by, 'twixt the fence and hedge - row,

Gold - en lan - tern bears on high, There's no hid - ing that glow.

Fier - y fai - ry by the trees, Give me your bright lan - tern, please!

The children stand in a loosely formed circle. Several children "fly" around the inside of the circle, making small gestures like fluttering wings. Then they use both hands to form the shape of a lantern and give it to another child standing close by. Now it is their turn to fly around the inside of the circle. Repeat until all the children have had a turn.

A Summer Feast

Words: M. Garff; Melody: F. Jaffke

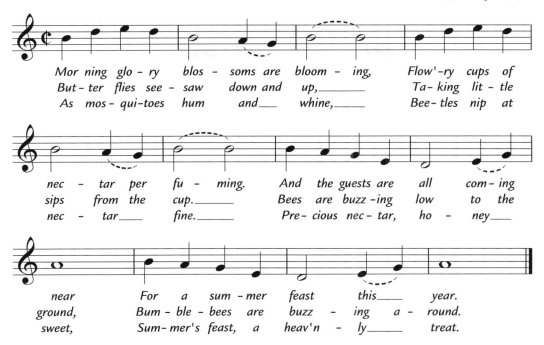

Mor - ning glo - ry blos - soms are bloom - ing, Flow'-ry cups of
But - ter flies see - saw down and up,_____ Ta - king lit - tle
As mos - qui-toes hum and___ whine,_____ Bee-tles nip at

nec - tar per fu - ming. And the guests are all com - ing
sips from the cup._____ Bees are buzz-ing low to the
nec - tar___ fine._____ Pre - cious nec - tar, ho - ney___

near For a sum - mer feast this___ year.
ground, Bum - ble - bees are buzz - ing a - round.
sweet, Sum-mer's feast, a heav'n - ly_____ treat.

Several children sit in the middle of the circle. They are the little flower cups. They form a flower with their hands. On verses 1 and 2, walk in a circle clockwise, holding hands. Everyone remains standing in a circle during the following verses, except for a small group of three or four children who will "fly" around the "flowers" in the middle. They carefully dip a hand into a flower cup and carry the "nectar" back to their place in the circle. Naturally, it would be fine to have all the children do the same movements together at the same time. This is probably a good idea if there are very few six-year-olds in the group.

The Midday Witch

Modified and expanded by Freya Jaffke from a verse by M. Garff

Little strawberry on a sunny hillside,
Drop of red, pretty as a picture,
Swinging along from side to side,
Here comes a gnome with a pitcher.
Little red berry, sweet as punch,
Ripe and good as a berry can be,
Perfect as a midday lunch,
For the gnome and his family. (M. GARFF)

During the next eight lines, the children walk around clockwise.
"Hold the pitcher" with the left hand and "pick the strawberry" with the right hand. The movement of bending to pick the berry should be done rhythmically.

… Stretched out upon a stepping-stone flat,
He takes a little nap.

Sit on the floor; set down the pitcher and lay head on folded hands in a gesture of sleep.

But around the hill someone is walking,
It's the Midday Witch who's stalking.
And when the little gnome she spied,
Do you know what she tried?
She cast a spell and quick as a flash,
Little gnome was a frog; into the pond — splash.

Walk with quiet, creeping steps.

Standing, make circles in the air with flat hands as a gesture of casting a spell. Hop like a frog.

Without a word, the Witch walked away,
Kept stalking around the hill at midday.
And when the little frog she spied,
Do you know what she tried?

Walk with quiet, creeping steps.

She cast a spell, would you believe,
Little frog was a bird and flew to a tree.

Standing, make circles in the air with flat hands as a gesture of casting a spell. "Fly around" with outspread arms.

Without a word, the Witch walked away,
Kept stalking around the hill at midday.
And when the little bird she spied,
Do you know what she tried?
She cast a spell, no sooner said,
The bird was a deer and into the forest sped.

Walk with quiet, creeping steps.

Standing, make circles in the air with flat hands as a gesture of casting a spell. Run and jump like a deer.

Without a word, the Witch walked away,
Kept stalking around the hill at midday.

Walk with quiet, creeping steps.

Little gnome woke up from his nap,
Rubbed his eyes and laughed and laughed;
After his restful midday repose,
He went straight home, just followed his nose;
Shared with the gnomes from his red strawberry,
Everyone had some and all were merry.

Sit on the floor with the gesture for sleep, as above.
Rub eyes and "laugh" by wiggling fingers.

Walk around in small gnome steps.
Everyone forms a bowl with two hands.
First an adult "shares" the strawberry,
then the children, if they wish to imitate the gesture.

DANCES

Come, Let's All Be Dancing

Melody: F. Jaffke

Come, let's all be danc - ing, danc - ing, danc - ing,

Clap - ping with our hands, Hi - ya - ya,

Clap - ping with our hands.

Vary bars 3 and 5 with the following words:

Stomp and stomp your foot,

Swim just like a fish,

Fly just like a bird,

Jump just like a frog,

And everyone holds hands,

Or:

Everyone stand still.

Everyone stands in a big, loosely formed circle.

On bars 1 and 2, with right hand raised in a gesture of asking someone to dance, turn around once.

On bars 3 and 5, do the corresponding movements while standing.

On bar 4, always clap lightly.

105

Johnny Fiddler

Melody: F. Jaffke

John - ny fid - dler, play for us, Child - ren would be dan - cing,

With their skirts so bright and full, Fringed a- round for pran - cing.

Dance with me, dance with me, With my a- pron white you see.

With me too, with me too, I've a snow - white a- pron too.

Several children stand in the middle of the circle as Johnny Fiddler.

Bars 1 – 8: All the children gesture as if playing the violin.

Bars 9 – 16: Each "Johnny Fiddler" chooses one child from the circle and dances with that child in the middle. The rest of the children clap lightly.

The ones who are chosen to dance, then remain in the middle and it starts over again.

Rumdiddle Dumdiddle

Melody: F. Jaffke

Rum - did - dle, Dum - did - dle, Doo - dle - doke,   Now we'll have a
Rum - did - dle, Dum - did - dle, Fee - dle - mouse,   Run - ning, run - ning

lit - tle joke.   Mu - sic plays for
through the house.   Mus - sic plays for

you to hear,   Car - ni - val comes once a year.
you to hear,   Car - ni - val comes once a year.

Holding hands, everyone walks around
in a long line.

107

Wooden Shoe Dance

Melody: F. Jaffke

When to Hol - land a trip we take, want - ing to boat on a

love - ly lake, There is the fish - er - man, his wife too, A -

swing - ing red skirts, her stock - ings blue. He has pant - a- loons like

skirts so wide, She wears pret - ty bon - nets all the time.

And what should they do,____ Wear - ing clogs for shoes?___

Danc - ing all the day__ with their wood - en shoe dance.

Bars 1 – 12: The children walk in pairs, side by side, around the circle clockwise.

Bars 13 – 14: Standing, using both hands, indicate the full skirt from front to back.

Bars 15 – 16: Stroke legs from ankles to knees to indicate stockings.

Bars 17 – 20: Indicate a full skirt with hands and also a bonnet on the head.

Bar 21: Clap.

Bar 22: With hands on hips, swing one foot forward and hop.

Bars 23 – 24: Couples dance holding hands.

The Jolly Jumper

Melody: F. Jaffke

We wan - der, we wan - der from here to o - ver yon - der. There's a jol - ly jump - er here, Shak - ing with her head, Rust - ling with her dress. Stamp - ing feet down low, Wav - ing us hel - lo. Danc - ing, dance, that's what we will, what we will, The oth - ers have to stand quite still.

Stand in a circle holding hands.

Bars 1 – 6: Several children go around the outside of the circle as the Jolly Jumper.

Bars 7 – 9: Two children make an opening in the circle and let the jumpers jump into the middle of the circle.

Bars 10 – 11: Shake your head.

Bars 12 – 13: Swish your skirt or shirt with both hands.

Bars 14 – 15: Lightly stomp with both feet.

Bars 16 – 17: Wave with one hand.

Bars 18 – 27: Each jumper takes one child from the circle and dances in the middle. The others lightly clap along.

Note: A different version of this song is available as "I Must Wander" in *The Singing, Playing Kindergarten* by Daniel Udo de Haes (WECAN).

Vida Vida Vit

German folk song

This game is for the older children. The younger ones like to sit in the middle and watch.

Walk in a circle holding hands for the first nine bars and then stand.

On "This is one time" put one foot forward and then back again. Then begin again. Repeat the movement for "This is one time" and add "this is two times" by putting first one foot and then the other, forward and back again. Then it starts over again. With every repetition another number is added, up to seven.

On:
"three times" – down on one knee
"four times" – down on one knee and then the other
"five times" – touch one elbow to the floor
"six times"– touch one elbow and then the other to
    the floor
"seven times" – touch nose to the floor

Index of Songs, Verses, and Games by First Line

Bibliography from the German Edition

We are grateful to all the publishers that gave permission for material to be reprinted.

Diestel, Hedwig. *Kindertag. Gedichte für Kinder,* seventh edition (Stuttgart, 1996).

Garff, Heiner and Marianne. *Fahr, mein Schifflein, fahre. Kinderlieder,* fourth edition (Stuttgart, 1995).

Garff, Marianne. *Es plaudert der Bach. Gedichte fuer Kinder* (Basel, 1996).

Garff, Marianne. *Pirzel und Purzel* (Bärenreiter Verlag, Kassel).

Künstler, Alois. *Das Brünnlein singt und saget. Lieder und Melodien für Kinder* (Stuttgart, 1994)

Martens, Heinrich. *Der Volkstanz,* Volume 14 (Vieweg Verlag, Berlin).

Morgenstern, Christian. *Liebe Sonne, liebe Erde. Ein Kinderliederbuch* (Oldenburg, 1984).

Ritter, Heinz, ed. *Eins und Alles. Gedichte für Kindheit und Jugend,* tenth edition (Stuttgart, 1998).

Rhythmen und Reime; Arbeitsmaterial aus den Waldorfkindergärten; Volume 6, eighth edition (Stuttgart, 2000).

Singspiele und Reigen; Arbeitsmaterial aus den Waldorfkindergärten, Volume 4, eighth edition (Stuttgart, 1998).

Further Reading

Collections of Songs, Verses, and Games

Foster, Nancy, ed. *Let Us Form a Ring*, (Acorn Hill, distributed by WECAN)

Foster, Nancy, ed. *Dancing as We Sing*, (Acorn Hill, distributed by WECAN)

Jaffke, Freya. *Play With Us: Social Games for Young Children* (WECAN, 2015)

Jones, Betty. *A Child's Seasonal Treasury* (Holon Press, distributed by WECAN, 2012)

Lonsky, Karen. *A Day Full of Song: Work Songs from A Waldorf Kindergarten*, Karen Lonsky (WECAN, 2009).

Russ, Johanne. *Clump-a-Dump and Snickle-Snack* (Mercury Press).

Seidenberg, Channa. *I Love to be Me* (Wynstones Press, 2002).

Willwerth, Ilian. *Merrily We Sing: Original Songs in the Mood of the Fifth* (WECAN, 2014).

The Wynstones Anthologies: *Autumn, Winter, Spring, Summer, Winter, Gateways, Spindrift* (Wynstones Press, 1999).

Background Information

Foster, Nancy, ed. *The Seasonal Festivals in Early Childhood: Seeking the Universally Human* (WECAN, 2010).

Jaffke, Freya. *Celebrating Festivals with Children* Freya Jaffke (Floris Books, 2011).

Pietzner, Carlo. *Festival Images for Today* (SteinerBooks, 2008).

Steiner, Rudolf, translated by Hans and Ruth Pusch. *The Calendar of the Soul* (SteinerBooks, 1988).

Steiner, Rudolf. *The Cycle of the Year as Breathing Process of the Earth* (Anthroposophic Press, 1998).

Steiner, Rudolf. *The Festivals and Their Meaning*, Rudolf Steiner (Rudolf Steiner Press, 2008).

Steiner, Rudolf. *The Four Seasons and the Archangels* (Rudolf Steiner Press, 2008).

Udo de Haes, Daniel. *The Singing, Playing Kindergarten* (WECAN, 2015).

About the Author

Freya Jaffke is a master Steiner/Waldorf kindergarten teacher and teacher trainer from Germany who has lectured and offered workshops for educators and parents in many countries. Her books on early childhood have sold over a quarter of a million copies worldwide, including *Toymaking with Children, Magic Wool, Celebrating Festivals with Children,* and *Work and Play in Early Childhood* (all Floris Books). A new translation of her classic book of games for early childhood, *Play with Us!* was recently published by WECAN.

She also edited and compiled *On the Play of the Child: Rudolf Steiner's Indications for Working with Young Children,* which was prepared as study material for the 2005 international Waldorf early childhood educators' conference. WECAN published the first English edition in 2006, and a second, revised and expanded edition in 2012.

Now retired, she continues to be active with marionette plays and teaching crafts and doll making at the Nikolas Cusanus House near Stuttgart.

Made in the USA
Monee, IL
21 July 2024

62417518R00066